THE
BASEBALL
CLINIC

THE BASEBALL CLINIC

John Stewart

BURFORD BOOKS

Printed in the United States of America

10 9 8 7 6 5 4 3 2 1

Library of Congress Cataloging-in-Publication Data

Stewart, John, 1964–
The baseball clinic / John Stewart.
        p.   cm.
    Includes index
    ISBN 1-58080-073-4 (pbk.)
    1. Baseball for children.   2. Baseball for children—Training.
  3. Baseball for children—Coaching.   I. Title.
  GV880.4.S84   1999
  796.37'62—dc21   98-51040
                                                                CIP

CONTENTS

This book is dedicated to my father,
John Stewart, Sr., for all of his hours of
hard work and perseverance teaching me
how to play this great game.

"Nothing's ever been as fun as baseball."
—Mickey Mantle
Yankee Outfielder

Introduction

Even as a very young boy, I dreamed of playing professional baseball. I watched the major league games on TV and studied all the players' moves. After the games I'd run outside, throw the ball against the garage, and imitate the actions I'd seen. I also played in the yard, hitting the ball as I tossed it in the air and running the bases even though nobody was in the field to catch the ball.

I spent many days playing baseball with my friends. No matter how many kids were present, we'd split up evenly—regardless of age—and play one-on-one, two-on two, or ten-on-ten. We'd play baseball in any vacant lot just as eagerly as on any field, making up the rules as we went along.

As I got older, I started to work out as well as play ball. Somewhere around the age of fifteen, I made it a practice on non-game days to run and lift light weights to improve my abilities.

Between my high school days and the start of college, I was offered a professional contract by the Chicago Cubs. I turned it down to further my education, though I continued to play baseball at the college level. At the end of my college career, I was drafted as a pitcher by the Atlanta Braves. Then came years of riding the bus, playing every night, and having the greatest time of my life playing for the AAA-level Richmond Braves—where I had reached the top of my ability. Every player, whether at the Little League or professional level, will find that his or her athletic career comes to an end—as did mine. Fortunately, because of my positive attitude and work ethic, instead of returning to my hometown and working at a more conventional job, I was asked to become a professional baseball scout for the Braves.

Today I travel the country, looking for talented young baseball players in high schools and colleges to whom I will offer a professional contract on behalf of the Braves organization.

I hope I'll someday stop at your field and give you the chance that I was given to play this glorious game. Above all, I hope this book helps you to play *your* best baseball and to get more enjoyment out of this great game.

—John Stewart
Granville, New York

A FEW WORDS ABOUT SPORTSMANSHIP AND ATTITUDE

The following pages will discuss proper mechanics, rules, scorekeeping, equipment, and many other aspects of the game of baseball. But no matter how much ability or desire a young player may have—one cannot overlook the value of good sportsmanship.

Good sportsmanship is the easiest ability to attain because you don't have to be a great baseball player to acquire it. It is an attribute that is essential, however, to becoming a role model or team leader.

What constitutes good sportsmanship? Of course, it means playing by the rules. But it also means hustling throughout the entire game, giving your team the best of your ability from start to finish, and maintaining an agreeable relationship with the umpire—even when you don't agree with his rulings.

Attitude is very similar to sportsmanship except that attitude has more to do with being positive toward your team, your teammates, and your own abilities. Keeping a positive attitude will help you play better because you truly believe you will be successful. Therefore, attitude can be one your greatest assets on the field.

Parents, fans, coaches, and scouts are very disappointed when they see a player throwing equipment, yelling at other players, or arguing with the umpire. Admirable among spectators and players alike, however, is the player who maintains a winning attitude no matter what the outcome of the game.

Good sportsmanship and attitude do not require you to be happy about losing—but they do require you to congratulate the victors and try harder to be successful the next time!

1

Warming Up

Stretching in preparation to play the game of baseball is essential. Baseball uses muscles and joints that are very small and easily injured. Most players, especially younger ones, find exercises boring and do very little to warm up prior to the game. This section will describe special stretches and warm-up techniques that will help a player loosen up and prevent serious injuries that can lead to missed games—or even end a career.

JOGGING & WIND SPRINTS

A light jog around the field is the first exercise you should conduct in your warm-up routine. One or two laps is sufficient to get the body heated up in preparation for muscle stretches.

Easy wind sprints are also an effective way to begin the warm-up. A wind sprint is a short run (40–60 yards) at full speed. An *easy* wind sprint is a run at half- to three-quarter speed. It is important not to push the leg muscles to attain full speed until the body has finished stretching.

TOE TOUCHES

This stretch will loosen your hamstrings (the back of the legs). Standing tall with your feet spread, bend at the hips and reach for your feet (toes). Bend *slowly*. The first few toe touches may evidence stiffness in your legs, so take your time and ease into the final toe touches.

JUMPING JACKS

Begin by standing upright with your feet together and your arms relaxed at your sides. Jump a few inches off the ground while opening your legs shoulder-width and touching your fingertips together overhead. Repeat the jump as you return to the original position. Continue in comfortably rapid succession.

SQUATS

Start this exercise by standing with your legs shoulder-width apart. Keeping the upper part of the body straight, bend at the knees to a complete crouch, then return to a standing position. This exercise will help loosen the back and all parts of the legs.

PECTORAL STRETCH

From a standing position, reach behind your body and try to touch your hands behind your back. If possible, clasp your hands behind you and lift your arms toward your shoulders. This will stretch the upper chest, an important preparation for throwing.

THE PECTORAL STRETCH

TRICEPS STRETCH

Outstretch your throwing arm into the air, keeping a bent elbow. Grasp the elbow with the other hand and firmly push the throwing arm toward the opposite shoulder. This will stretch the

THE TRICEPS STRETCH

back of the arm called the triceps. This muscle is central to the throwing action.

SHOULDER SHRUGS

This exercise will help to loosen your shoulder muscles. Stand with your arms at your sides. Lift your shoulders (only) and attempt to squeeze your neck with the tops of your shoulders. Hold this position briefly, then relax once more. Repeat ten to fifteen times.

ARM CIRCLES

This motion will stretch the small muscles in the shoulders. Stand with your arms outstretched at your sides, assuming the position of a "T." Start by moving your arms in small, controlled circles and slowly increase the range of motion until the circles are very large. When the arms tire, rest; then begin again.

BACK STRETCH

Lay on the ground and lift your feet over your head. Pause and then slowly return your feet to the ground. This will stretch your back and your neck.

BACK STRETCH

GROIN STRETCH

Stand with your feet far apart. With your hands on your hips, bend at the right knee and ease your body to the right, *slowly* shifting your weight over the bent knee. Do not bounce on your knee as the groin muscle will injure easily. Hold this position for five seconds. Return to the start position and repeat the exercise over the left knee. Continue this sequence until muscles are loose.

GROIN STRETCH

HAMSTRING STRETCH

Sit on the ground with your legs straight out and together. Reach forward with your hands and touch your toes. If possible, hold your feet for a few seconds. Repeat ten times. An advanced form of this exercise is to hold your feet and bend your head to touch your knees. Don't worry if this is not possible for you to do in the beginning. With practice, you will attain greater flexibility and range of motion.

TRUNK TWISTS

Stand with your hands on your hips and your legs spread shoulder-width. Rotate your upper body left and right in a spinning motion. This will loosen the muscles in your back, sides, and stomach.

FOREARM STRETCH

Reach one arm out in front of you with the palm up. Use the other hand to grasp the fingers of the outstretched hand. Slowly pull the fingers toward the body. This will stretch the muscles of the forearm which are important to throwing the ball. Be sure to stretch these muscles slowly so as not to pull them.

FOREARM STRETCH

QUADRICEPS STRETCH

Stand with your feet together. Bend one knee and lift your leg. Grasp the ankle and gently pull upward. This should produce some tension at the front of the leg. Repeat, using the other leg. Be careful not to lose your balance.

CALF RAISES

Stand with your feet together. Slowly shift your weight onto your toes, hold, and then return your heels to the ground. Repeat 15–20 times.

QUADRICEPS STRETCH

Warming up may seem monotonous and barely worthwhile, but given how important health and fitness are to the baseball player, these ten minutes can save a career. Be sure to take your time and execute the movements correctly. Do not begin throwing the ball until the body is completely warm and loose. It will serve you to establish a warm-up routine and complete this routine before every game. If the weather is cold or wet, occasional stretches between innings are also advisable.

The following chapters will recommend stretches and suggest a warm-up routine for each position. Remember, you can never loosen too much!

2

Pitching

The Warm-Up

Warm-up for a pitcher is probably the most important aspect of the game. Without it, injury is nearly guaranteed. A rule of thumb for loosening is: *Warm-up to throw, do not throw to warm-up.* This means instead of throwing to work up a sweat, do some light exercises and run to get your body warm before throwing.

On the day you are scheduled to pitch, be sure to bring a jacket and a spare undershirt to the ballpark. You'll also need to bring a towel and water (if your team does not provide them).

Pre-Game

Perform the following warm-up exercises prior to taking the mound to pitch the game. You do not necessarily have to practice these step-by-step, but establish a routine that you can follow every game. Doing so will help you to focus on the business at hand.

1. Take a light jog, do easy wind sprints, or perform jumping jacks to get the blood flowing and loosen the legs.

2. Do some leg stretches, toe touches, squats, etc. Limber legs are a must for pitching so be sure to stretch them well.

3. Do arm, pectoral, and triceps stretches; shoulder shrugs and arm circles. Arms consist of many small muscles that can easily tear if not completely loosened.

4. Now begin to throw lightly, concentrating on proper arm action and finish. Good habits carry over into play—always practice as if you were in a game.

5. Ask a catcher to toss with you from his catching position (squatting) to establish your release point and proper mechanics.

6. Do not immediately throw full speed. Gradually throw harder until you are completely loose; ten to fifteen minutes should be sufficient.

7. When completely loose, put your jacket on and sit in the dugout. Do not wear a jacket when throwing. The purpose of the jacket is to maintain a sweat—not to produce one.

During a game, a pitcher is allowed eight pitches between innings. Be sure to take all the allotted throws and perform them as if they were part of the game. Standing on the mound and lightly tossing the ball home will not loosen you up, nor will it help you to keep your rhythm.

About halfway through the game, especially when it is very hot, change your dampened undershirt. A wet shirt can become cold and cause tendonitis. If possible, bring an undershirt with sleeves that reach below the elbow. A shirt that only covers the biceps leaves the elbow exposed and could lead to elbow stiffness later in the game.

The Mechanics of Pitching

The mechanics of pitching are the most important part of your position. Without proper mechanics a player will never reach his full potential. He will be injury-prone and slow to recover—and most of all—he will struggle with control.

The actions described below cover the mechanics of pitching from wind-up through the finish, and assume **a right-handed pitcher.**

1. **Address the hitter.** This simply means to stand on the rubber with both feet facing the catcher. This is the first movement in the pitching wind-up.

2. **Clear the rubber** by stepping back with the foot opposite your throwing hand (in this case, the left foot). The step does not need to be large. Actually, the smaller the step, the easier it is to keep your balance (see Figure 1). You are now into your wind-up.

Figure 1

3. **Turn the front (right) foot** into the hole located directly in front of the rubber. The foot must remain in contact with the rubber or a "balk" (an illegal pitch) can be called. Your body is now in position to gather leverage (see Figure 2).

Figure 2

4. **Pick up the foot behind the rubber.** This will require you to balance on your turned foot (now the back foot). The more leverage you can gather at this point, the greater the opportunity to produce velocity. A larger, longer-limbed pitcher has the advantage here, so it becomes

even more important for a smaller player to become compact and explosive in his wind-up and delivery.

As you can see, Figure 3 shows excellent balance as well as very compact form. The height of the leg kick is not extremely important, but depends upon how long the pitcher needs to get his arm in the throwing position. At the top of your leg kick you should take the ball out of your glove and begin to get it into the throwing position.

Figure 3

5. **Sweep the ball down below your waist** (see Figure 4) **and then back over your head** in a circular motion (see Figure 5). At this point the wind-up is complete. The remainder of the pitching action is called the "follow through" or "finish."

Loaded position

Figure 4

Figure 5
The stride

6. **Return the suspended foot to the ground** in a striding action toward the plate. It

17

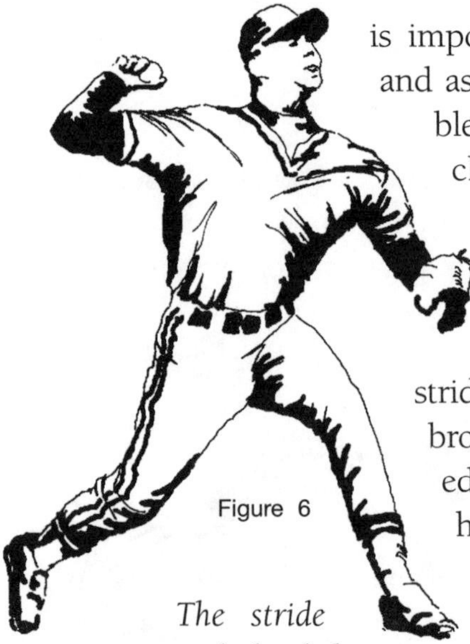

is important to try to stride comfortably and as directly toward the plate as possible. Try to land with your foot slightly closed (pointed slightly toward the hitter as opposed to the catcher) and on its ball. During the stride, the arm should be brought into the "loaded" position over your head as illustrated in Figure 5.

Figure 6

The stride and loaded position should occur at the same time. Many problems can and will occur if the rhythm is not smooth at this point.

Figure 7

7. **As the landing foot hits the ground, thrust your throwing arm forward** to release the ball toward the plate. The following figures clarify the release point and finish of the pitching motion: Figure 6 shows proper positioning of the chest and head at the point of release. Notice that the body is well-balanced and centered over the front leg;

Figure 8

Figure 7 reveals good extension and hip rotation for the release; Figure 8 shows the back leg following through to complete the pitching motion.

Notice that throughout this series of movements, all pitchers have maintained excellent balance. The next few pages will break down the most common problems leading to imbalance and a loss of velocity or control.

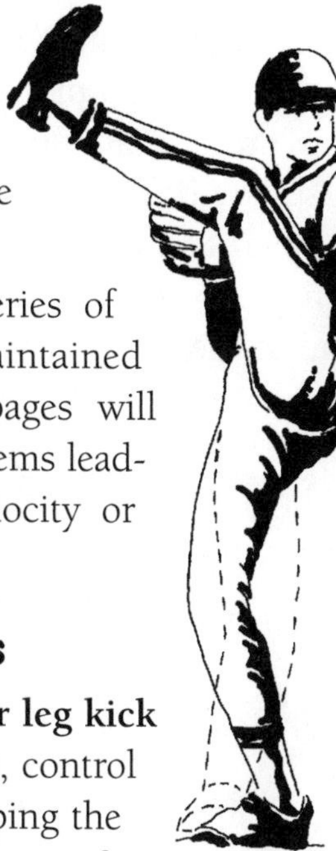

Common Problems

Poor balance at the top of your leg kick results in a loss of velocity, and often, control problems. This is easily fixed by keeping the shoulders, hips, and head centered on top of each other, thereby staying upright during the wind-up. In Figure 9, the pitcher's balance is well forward of the back drive leg.

Figure 9
Correct knee position

Rolling over on the landing foot is common to pitchers who "fly open." Flying open means the pitcher throws his shoulders at the plate before it's time to throw. This normally causes extreme control problems and terrible balance, as seen in Figure 10.

Figure 10
"Flying open"

Upper body tilt is also very common, especially to

overhand throwers. As seen in Figure 11 the pitcher's upper body is falling away from home plate. This usually causes the ball to be up in the strike zone.

Earlier, in Figure 7, we saw a pitcher with proper positioning of the chest and head at the point of release. In Figure 12, however, we see a pitcher who did not get his body over the landing leg. This does not often affect control—but does decrease velocity due to reduced leverage.

Figure 11
Upper body tilt

Two more common problems are **overstriding** and **landing on your heel.** Both of these problems, as shown in Figure 13, are easy to correct through practice drills, but if they are not addressed, they can lead to arm and control problems.

Landing on a stiff front leg (see Figure 14) is a frequent problem that can lead to back and arm trouble—and is often not correctable.

Figure 12

Of course, there are many more problems that can occur during the pitching motion. Given that every pitcher is different and not everyone throws the same, what works for one player may not work for another. The mechanics explained here are the major ones that should be taught and practiced.

Figure 13

Figure 14

Aside from these mechanical problems, younger players are especially vulnerable to issues that stem from failing to warm-up properly, throwing on an irregular schedule, or overusing their pitching arm. Caution and common sense are the watchwords here.

Also, inexperienced and younger pitchers sometimes struggle to withstand the mental demands of their position. It helps if they are reminded to keep their eyes on the catcher during the wind-up and follow though, and to maintain their concentration. Most of all, younger pitchers need to bear in mind (especially in the wake of a poorly thrown ball) that every pitch is a new throw…forget the poor pitch, concentrate on the mechanics, and above all, think positive!

Practice Drills

DRY DRILLS

These are very easy to do and do not require another person's assistance. Find a pitching mound at the local playground and practice the wind-up with no ball or catcher. It is very important to use your glove and wear spikes. Run through the motion many times at different speeds to get comfortable with all the movements and activities required during the wind-up. Experiment with many different strides and leg kicks to find a comfortable rhythm. The advantage of dry drills is that you can practice the wind-up without wearing out your arm or risking injury.

THE BUCKET DRILL

The bucket drill will help you break the habit of leg sweeping. A leg sweeper is a pitcher who swings his leg to the plate instead of striding directly at the plate. (Figure 15, at left, is correct, while the pitcher at right is incorrect.) A leg sweeper may

Figure 15

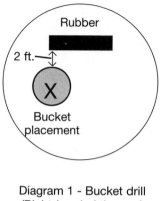

Diagram 1 - Bucket drill
(Right-handed thrower)

not have any real mechanical problems, but correcting the habit could add speed to the fastball.

To perform this drill, start on the mound. Place a five-gallon bucket on the throwing-hand side of the rubber, two feet toward the plate (see Diagram 1). Practice your wind-up and follow through, paying special attention not to kick the bucket. Repeat this drill until the habit is broken.

TOE DOWN DRILL

This drill will help the player with an overstriding or heel-landing problem. When running through the wind-up, point your toe down when you pick up your front leg. This technique will force you to shorten your stride and enable you to land on the ball of your foot. This drill has also been used to help correct a leg sweep.

GUIDE LINES

Before starting to pitch off the mound, stand at the base of the hill facing centerfield. Walk up the mound toward the rubber. Find the center of the rubber and, using your foot, scratch a line directly toward the plate about six feet long. Run through your wind-up and follow through, paying attention to where your lead foot lands. Ideally, the foot should be on

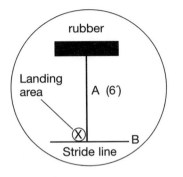

**Diagram 2 - Guide lines
(Right-handed thrower)**

the line or slightly inclined to the throwing side. The "X" in Diagram 2 pinpoints the proper landing area for a right-handed pitcher. If your lead foot crosses Line A, you are flying open. Note that the landing area can vary three-to-four inches in either direction. Line B in the diagram is the stride line. This is measured by starting at the middle of the rubber and walking toe-to-heel down the mound until you reach the footprint of your landing foot. Be sure to measure this distance after you have thrown a good strike. (Measuring after a poor throw may lead to repeated misthrows.) After measuring the distance, draw a horizontal line at the top of your footprint to form your stride line. From now on, your stride should find your toe just barely touching the line. This drill is extremely helpful when a pitcher is experiencing control problems or has an inconsistent stride.

STATUE DRILL

This drill helps a pitcher to establish balance. Start by running a dry drill. At the very top of the leg kick, pause and hold this position. If you cannot hold this position for at least a split second, you are rushing. Mastering this drill will enable you to develop maximum balance and leverage—which results in greater velocity.

LONG TOSS DRILL

There is no better drill to increase your velocity than the long toss. The drill is very simple. Find a partner and loosen up slowly. As you get loose, gradually step backward until you can no longer reach your partner with maximum effort. Continue to throw for a period of time (approximately twenty minutes). Although long toss in the off-season is a great training tool, it's hard to throw long toss with any great extent when you have to pitch twice a week. The chart below will help you to schedule your long toss during the playing season. A quick long toss is not ruled out when warming up on game day.

Long Toss Chart

game day - short period of long toss (5–10 minutes)

day after   - run distance, get sweaty

next day   - light long toss and sprints

third day   - light long toss and running, throw off mound for control

fourth day - run, run, run,

fifth day   - time to pitch again

Fielding The Position

If a pitcher has practiced the mechanics we've covered in the previous pages—and mastered them—fielding should be easy. The most important part of fielding your position is balance. Without balance a pitcher will struggle with eye-hand coordination which is essential to fielding balls. With proper finish, a pitcher should be facing the plate, ready to jump on ground balls hit toward him. Here is a list of the important mechanics of fielding from the mound.

1. Quick feet: Move with short, quick steps at the ball. A player using long strides will find it hard to react to a bad hop or a ball carrying "English" (a spinning action). Also, if a runner is taking an extra base, the pitcher taking long strides will be slow to position his body for the throw.

2. Bend at the knee: As you attack the ball, be sure to flex at the knees instead of at the waist. If you bend at the waist only, you are farther from the ball and will be more inclined to take your eyes away from it to prepare for the throw. Bending at the waist also requires more time to get the ball and throw it to the base. (Infielders also fall prey to this problem.)

3. Set feet: Plant your feet firmly under your body. Ninety-five percent of misthrown balls are the result of throwing off-balance. If possible, after fielding the ball, take a short step toward the base and then throw. This short step is called a "crow hop." When there is not time to step and throw, use extra concentration and don't take your eyes off the target. When playing in wet condi-

tions, using a third finger on the ball when throwing will help to prevent a misthrow.

4. The stopped ball: When fielding a bunt or "slow roller" that has stopped do not use your glove, use your bare hand. The ball is easily lost in the glove and often falls out when there is no velocity.

5. Listen: Be aware of other fielders. The slow rollers are often fielded by the wrong player. As a pitcher heads for the ball he is moving farther away from the bases and has his back to the play. Be alert and listen, because the third baseman or catcher may be able to make the play much more easily than you can. They will also tell you where to throw if they are unable to make the play themselves.

6. Throw correctly: Make throws overhand if possible. Most poorly thrown balls to the bases are the result of sidearm throws or underhand tosses. Unless an emergency situation arises, set your feet and throw the ball overhand.

Philosophy

Regardless of the pitcher's mechanics, velocity, or fielding ability, there is no defense for a walk. For a coach or player, there is no worse feeling than to see the other team get baserunners from walks (which usually end a pitcher's game). Throwing strikes is a pitcher's most important job—he must concentrate on the catcher's glove and forget the hitter, umpire, and fans!

The reality is, most hitters have success *less than three out of ten times at bat.* You, the pitcher, must not let anyone see you upset or struggling with your game. You must continue to work on mechanics and balance, keeping in mind that fielders' errors and hits are out of your control. Strikes will keep you in the game!

3

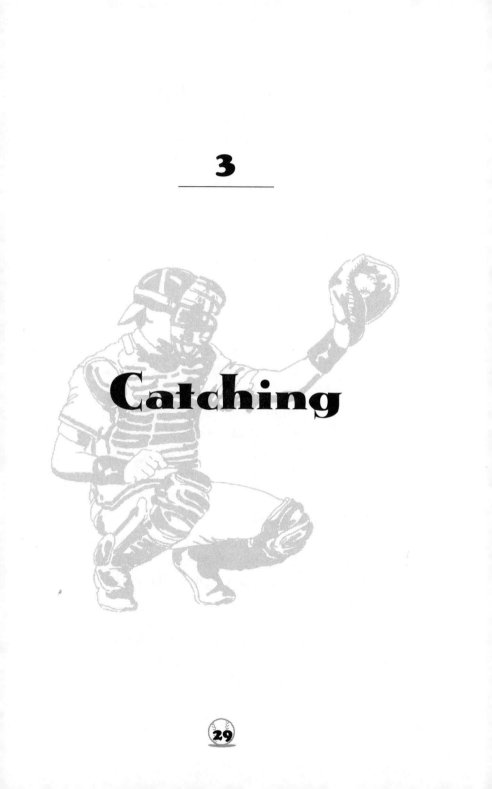

Catching

The Warm-Up

As with every other position in baseball, pre-game loosening is essential. For a catcher, the two most important body parts are the arms and legs. A catcher cannot shift to block balls or back up bases on a hit ball if he has a leg injury. And if a catcher has an injured arm, he will be unable to throw out would-be base stealers. The following exercises will help you get loose before the game.

1. Take a light jog around the field to loosen the body and stretch the legs.

2. Do toe touches, groin, and hamstring stretches to loosen the legs.

3. Do trunk twists to loosen the back and sides, arm circles to work the shoulders, and triceps and forearm stretches to loosen the arms.

4. Once you are fully stretched and prepared to throw, do wind sprints to help you work up a sweat.

5. Start playing toss and gradually increase your distance and velocity until fully loose. Long toss, as discussed in the section on pitching, is a great way to finish loosening your throwing arm.

When all of these exercises are complete, you're ready to take the infield with the rest of the team. The whole series of stretches should take no more than fifteen minutes.

The catcher may be the most important player on the field. He runs the team. The infield depends on him to position them from hitter to hitter. Without his leadership behind the plate, a team is at a severe disadvantage. The pitcher depends on him to keep balls in play and keep him focused

Tools of the Trade

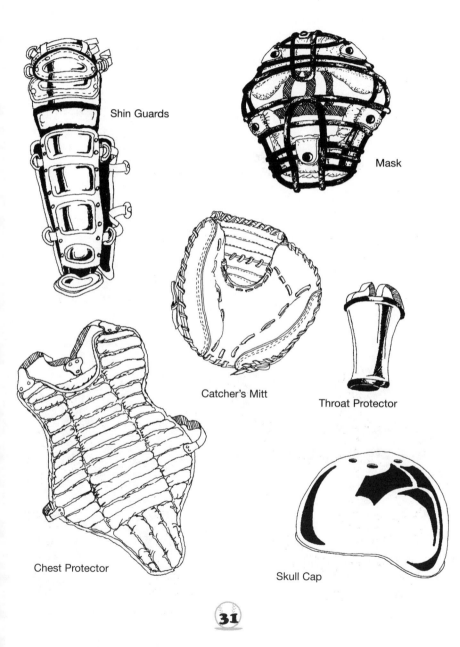

Shin Guards

Mask

Catcher's Mitt

Throat Protector

Chest Protector

Skull Cap

on the strike zone. A good catcher may also assist the pitcher with mechanical problems.

The following pages will help you become a mechanically sound player behind the plate. Outstanding physical ability is an asset, but many players catching in the major leagues have very average tools with outstanding mechanics. Catching may be the only position in baseball which can be learned and mastered well enough to carry you to the big leagues. All other positions require above-average tools.

The Mechanics of Catching

THE STANCE

When behind the plate a catcher's playing position is the squat. Most catchers squat incorrectly and this limits their mobility. In a proper squat, your legs are shoulder-width apart and your feet are pointed toward the base lines. You should be resting on the balls of your feet, with your weight

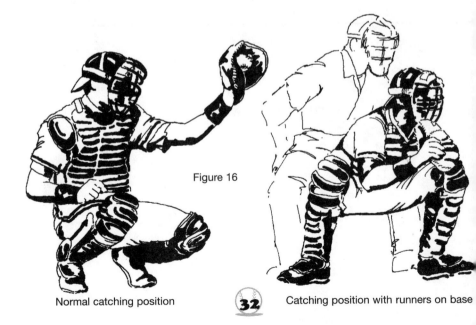

Figure 16

Normal catching position

Catching position with runners on base

over your knees. You should be facing the pitcher with your knees aligned parallel to the pitching rubber, as seen in Figure 16. One of the most common faults in the catching position is having your feet staggered. This limits your lateral movement.

To check if your stance is staggered, look at the position of your knees when squatting. Instead of being aligned parallel to the rubber, one knee will be slightly ahead of the other.

The catcher should position himself under the back shoulder of the hitter, close enough to almost touch him should he reach up. This may seem too close, but a hitter strides forward to hit, thereby increasing his distance from the catcher. Figure 16 shows the proper stance to receive the ball.

FRAMING

Framing is the art of catching the thrown ball with as little effort and as softly as possible, creating the illusion that most pitches are strikes. This is an outstanding technique that, when mastered, will greatly improve your catching. When you are first learning to frame, it's important to understand the strike zone and how to handle pitches that are in or around it. Framing entails taking the square strike zone and rounding the edges, as illustrated in Diagram 3.

It's also important for you to envision the strike zone as a clock. The top of the strike zone is twelve o'clock and the bottom of the zone is six o'clock. Now, round off the strike zone as shown in Diagram 4, making the outside corner three o'clock and the inside corner nine o'clock (based on a right-

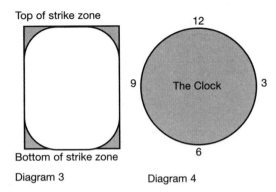

Diagram 3

Diagram 4

handed hitter). The palm of the catcher's mitt should always face the middle of the plate. Low pitches are received with palm up, and high pitches are caught with palm down. Outside pitches as well as inside pitches are caught with palm in, as seen in Diagram 5.

CATCHING THE BALL

The ball should be caught with a slightly bent elbow. This will allow the arm to "give" as the ball enters the mitt. A stiff elbow at the point of reception can cause the ball to bounce out of the glove. You should also catch all balls—regardless of whether they are strikes or balls—inside the body. Catching a ball "inside the body" means to receive the pitch inside the shoulders. This helps to create the illusion of a strike, even when a ball is slightly out of the strike zone. Although you've already learned how to frame balls thrown around the parameters of the strike zone, it is not necessary to frame balls well out of the strike zone. These pitches should simply be caught.

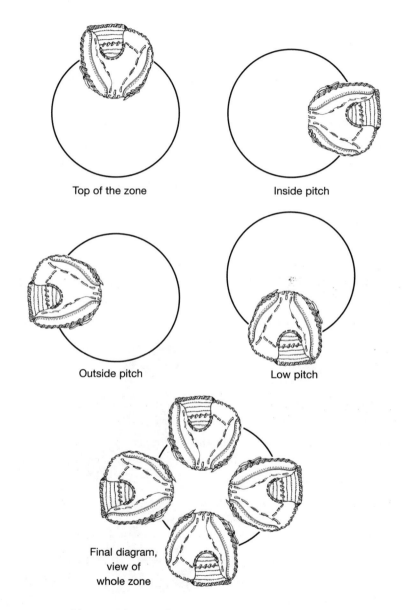

Top of the zone

Inside pitch

Outside pitch

Low pitch

Final diagram,
view of
whole zone

Diagram 5 (as seen from mound, to right-handed hitter)

SHIFTING

Shifting is a technique used to get your body in position to frame the ball. This is an easy skill to learn and will increase the likelihood that balls thrown out of the strike zone will be called strikes.

When the pitch is in the air, smoothly drift toward the area where it will bypass the batter. Do not jump in that direction or shift too quickly. Observe the ball's flight and as you prepare to frame it, glide toward the ball.

BLOCKING BALLS

The act of blocking keeps poorly thrown balls from getting past the catcher, enabling a runner to advance. Starting in the squat, a catcher's first move is to glide left or right depending on the direction of the pitch. As you approach the area where you believe the ball will enter the catching box, drop to one knee in the direction of the ball and relax your body. If a ball is thrown to your left, the left knee is dropped to the ground. If the ball is to your right, drop to the right knee (see Figure 17). You must relax your body to cut down on the ricochet should the ball hit your chest. If the ball strikes your body while you are tense, the stiff muscles will allow the

Figure 17
Blocking balls

ball to bounce a great distance. A relaxed body will tend to accept the ball softly, resulting in a smaller ricochet.

While on one knee, with your body relaxed, try to round your shoulders to keep the ball in front of you—rather than allowing it to bounce to the side. To round your shoulders, drop your hands between your legs with palms up and elbows pointed out. This will shift your shoulders forward and drop your upper chest backward while creating a pocket-like half-circle from shoulder to shoulder. The final tip to help you block balls correctly is to keep your back straight. This will expose more of your chest and give you more body-blocking area (see Figure 17).

THROWING TO THE BASES

Another responsibility of the catcher is to throw out base stealers. The ideal catcher has a strong throwing arm, but a quick, accurate release is equally as important. If a catcher with a poor arm can master the quick, accurate throw, he can be just as effective. When throwing to a base, the most important mechanic is footwork. Poor footwork accounts for most poorly thrown balls.

Prepare to throw by planting your feet. As the ball is in flight toward the plate, pivot your right foot by pointing the right knee out. This cocks your hips and will enable you to throw with velocity. Next, catch the ball and point your front shoulder at the target while transferring the ball to your ungloved hand. As you transfer the ball, your momentum should shift toward the target. When the ball is firmly gripped your ungloved hand, raise the ball into the loaded position (see Figure 18). Remember, a quick release is impor-

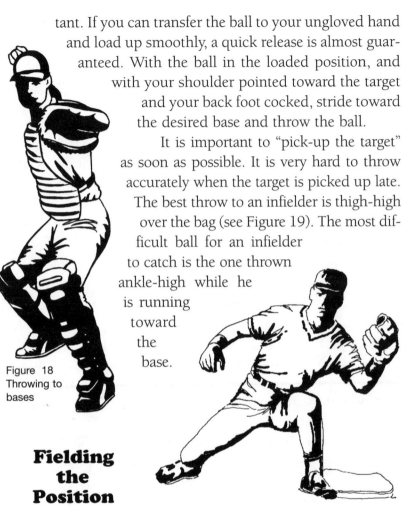

tant. If you can transfer the ball to your ungloved hand and load up smoothly, a quick release is almost guaranteed. With the ball in the loaded position, and with your shoulder pointed toward the target and your back foot cocked, stride toward the desired base and throw the ball.

It is important to "pick-up the target" as soon as possible. It is very hard to throw accurately when the target is picked up late.

The best throw to an infielder is thigh-high over the bag (see Figure 19). The most difficult ball for an infielder to catch is the one thrown ankle-high while he is running toward the base.

Figure 18
Throwing to bases

Figure 19

Fielding the Position

Normally a catcher is in charge of directing traffic and there are few plays he needs to worry about making himself. Among the plays a catcher does need to field, however, are the swinging bunt and the sacrifice bunt.

The first step in making either of these plays is to remove the mask. Be sure to clear the mask from the area, tossing it in the direction opposite to the play. The next step is to move quickly toward the ball, using short strides. Long strides will make it harder to adjust to bad hops or a ball with English. Do not attempt to glove the ball. The glove should be placed on the far side of the ball to stop it from rolling. Using your bare hand, pick up the ball. Now, plant your feet, point your front shoulder toward the target, and throw to the base.

The only other play we will cover here is the "pop-up." This is one of the hardest plays in baseball for many reasons. The first difficulty is "picking-up" (that is, spotting) the ball. With your mask on and your back to the play, you must rely on the pitcher's guidance. As you become more experienced with this play, you will be able to judge the flight of the ball with less assistance.

Just as you do with the bunt, remove the mask and hold on to it until you've spotted the ball. Then throw the mask in the direction opposite to the play. Now pursue the ball, keeping in mind that the ball has backspin. This backspin will cause the ball to drift back toward the mound. While judging the pop-up ball, turn your back to the playing field so that when the ball starts to drift it will return to you—much like a Frisbee (see

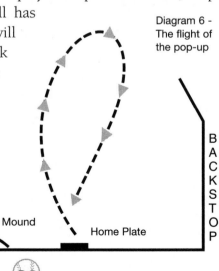

Diagram 6 - The flight of the pop-up

Pitcher's Mound

Home Plate

BACKSTOP

Diagram 6). Be sure to keep your feet moving throughout this activity. If you become stationary, any small adjustment will throw off your judgment. Be sure to yell, "I got it," to let the other players know you are prepared to catch the ball.

BACKING UP

If there is no play to be made at the plate, a catcher can back up the bases. On every ground ball to the infield, a catcher can hustle down the line toward the first base dugout to stop the overthrown ball to first base. On a double with no runners on, he can step up to the bag and cover first base if the runner decides to come back to first (see Diagram 7).

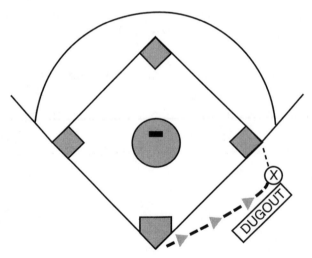

Diagram 7 Backup route

BE IN CHARGE

As a catcher's skill level increases, so must his leadership on the diamond. A catcher has to "keep the pitcher in the game." The pitcher has to concentrate on many aspects of the game while he is pitching—but he also has his back to the game. The catcher, in essence, functions as the pitcher's eyes and ears, informing him of the activity taking place behind the mound. Of course, the catcher is also involved in every pitch. He knows more about how the ball is moving or how much velocity is on the pitch. The catcher must keep the lines of communication open, helping the pitcher to stay calm, formulate a plan of attack, and stay focused on throwing strikes. Baseball is a team sport, and the pitcher/catcher team is the most important one on the field.

What's more, a catcher must position the players in the field and direct traffic on pop-ups. A catcher should be aware of the outs, the count on the hitter, and where the batter likes to hit the ball—all this in addition to being able to play his

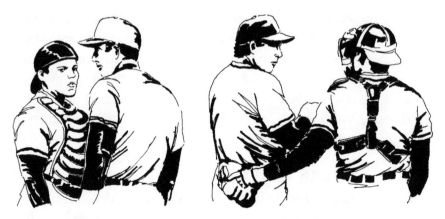

Figure 20   Figure 21

position. Figures 20 and 21 show a catcher keeping a pitcher in the game.

Practice Drills

REBOUND FRAMING

It is ideal to have a pitcher throw to you when you practice framing. This drill, however, can be done without any assistance.

Find a flat wall with at least fifteen feet of clearance. Squat in the catcher's position, ten feet away from and facing the wall. Throw the ball against the wall with enough velocity for it to rebound on a flat plane, similar to a pitched ball. Using the techniques covered in this chapter, shift and frame the ball. Concentrate on the mechanics. This is a great way to get comfortable with the art of receiving the ball.

BLOCKING DRILL

For this drill you'll need a full set of equipment. Before starting, be sure to stretch your legs well. Have a partner stand twenty feet away with a handful of balls. Get into the catching position, facing your partner. Your partner should now toss balls at you, "short-hopping" every throw. Make sure he allows you enough time to get settled between throws. Work hard on your mechanics; push yourself to catch every ball.

GROUNDERS DRILL

It may sound crazy, but fielding grounders with the catcher's mitt is a good way to work on "soft hands." The only way to get better at using the mitt is to catch balls at many different angles. Occasionally, while the infielders are taking grounders, jump in and field a handful of hits.

4

First Base

The Warm-Up

Every position has its own stretching routine, specially designed for the body parts that are most important to that position. For the first baseman, the legs are of utmost importance. The first baseman's primary job is to catch or stop every thrown ball. He may have to outstretch his body along the base line when trying to catch the ball—while keeping his foot on the bag. Here is a routine to help you get loose before the game.

1. Take a light jog around the field to warm the body and stretch the legs.
2. Do toe touches, and groin and hamstring stretches. These will also stretch the legs.
3. Stretch the quadriceps and do calf raises. Repeat some groin and hamstring exercises.
4. Do some wind sprints now that you are warm and your legs are loose.
5. Play some toss and catch to loosen the arms and shoulders.

When these exercises are complete, you are ready to take the infield. Between innings, while throwing the ball around the infield, be sure to continue stretching the legs. It's easy to suffer leg injuries at first base, which, in turn, could cause you to miss games. A couple of stretches between innings will decrease the likelihood of injury.

Playing First Base

First base is one of the easier positions to play in baseball. Usually, the player at first base is in the lineup to produce offense. There are some techniques you can use at first base to improve your defensive play, but often, coaches do not spend time on them, thinking all a first baseman has to do is catch the throws.

FIELDING GROUNDERS

Much like every other infield position, first base requires that you catch ground balls. One advantage the first baseman has over the rest of the infield is that he can knock the ball down in an emergency instead of catching it cleanly. Because he is so close to the bag, he has more time to field the ball. The proper mechanics of fielding grounders is covered in detail in chapter 5: Playing Middle Infield.

THROWING TO BASES

Should there be a runner on base, you may have to throw the ball. Set your feet, point your front shoulder toward the target, stride, and throw the ball. The most common play is a grounder to first base with a runner already on first. In this case, the first thing you must do is "clear the runner." Clearing the runner is done by stepping forward or backward one step after successfully catching the ball. This step will enable you to throw around the runner cleanly, while also allowing the middle infielder to see the ball. It is too difficult to throw the ball *over* the runner. Nine out of ten times, the ball strikes the runner in the back. If—by chance—the ball does get by the runner, the middle infielder is sure to miss it because he never got a good look at it.

Sometimes, in an effort to catch the grounder, you'll find yourself too far from first base to beat the runner. In this situation, use an underhand toss to throw the ball to either the pitcher or the second baseman covering first base. Just as you would when throwing overhand, you must set your feet. Get a firm grip on the ball and take it out of your glove. If you leave the ball in the glove too long, a player running to cover the base will have to struggle to see the ball being thrown. Next, give the ball a firm underhand toss, much like pitching a kickball. If you decide to take the ball to the base yourself, yell, "I got it" to call off the other infielders. Failing to do so may result in a traffic jam at first base and increase the chance that someone will get hurt.

FOOTWORK

The best defensive skill a first baseman can possess is good footwork around the base. A player with good footwork will salvage many poor throws and keep runners from advancing an extra base.

When preparing to catch a ball thrown to first base, you must start by straddling the base. Do this by placing one foot on each side of the base in fair territory, facing second. Now you must judge to which side of the base the ball is being thrown. The side the ball is thrown to will determine which side of the bag must remain in contact with your foot. For example, if the second baseman throws the ball to the out-field-side of first, your foot must stay in contact with the right side of the base. If the ball is thrown to the home-plate side of first, keep your foot on the left side. (Diagram 8 shows the contact point for both throws.)

Regardless of which side of the base is the contact point, use the same foot to maintain contact. If you are a right-

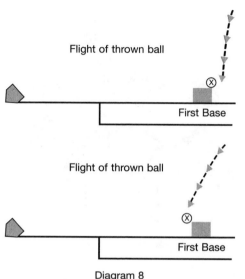

Flight of thrown ball

First Base

Flight of thrown ball

First Base

Diagram 8
⊗ indicates foot position

handed player, use the right foot. If you are left-handed, use the left foot. Some players make the mistake of alternating the contact foot according to the direction of the throw. This will cause you to reach across your body and limit the extension of your gloved hand. The only good cause for using the alternate foot is in the event of a bunt. When a catcher has to throw to you, he will yell "inside" or "outside" to direct you to the side of the base that is his target. Here, you will use the foot closest to the foul line. If the catcher yells "inside," you will use your left foot. If he says "outside," you will use your right foot. Your feet, regardless of the contact point, should never be in the middle of the base as a runner will spike or run over you. It is important to provide a good target to all throwers. Be sure to clear the runner to make yourself more visible. (Figure 22 shows the first baseman receiving the ball from the catcher incorrectly. He did not clear the runner.)

Your main job is to keep the ball in play. If that means leaving the base, do it. You must also stop all balls to keep runners from advancing another base.

Occasionally a throw will be high and you must jump off the base to catch it. As you return to the bag after catching the ball, sweep the glove down the base-line to tag the runner. Obviously, if you have enough time to land on the base ahead of the runner, the tag is not necessary.

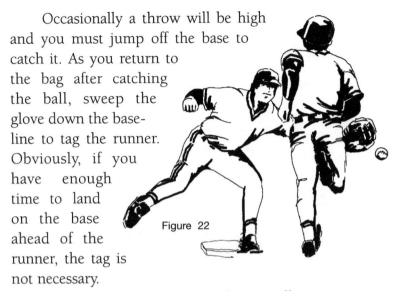

Figure 22

On high throws that you know will require you to jump, get more height by starting your jump from the top of the base. Standing on top of the base will give you an additional three- to four-inch lift.

Cutoffs

Another play a first baseman is involved in is the cutoff from an outfielder. Here, his job is to catch the ball, if needed, and relay it to the base being attempted by the runner. Many different styles of cutoffs are used, depending on the coach, so we will only discuss the proper mechanics of receiving and unloading the ball on a cutoff play. Run full speed to the area designated for the cutoff. If you do not get to the area quickly, you may have to catch the ball on the run, which is very difficult. Square up to the outfielder, making it easy to see the ball and the outfield. Raise your hands high

over your head so the outfielder
can easily see you. Now, listen to
the infielder you will be throwing to.
He will position you in line with the
base. As the ball is in flight, pivot your
foot to open your hips and enable a quick-
er release. This is done by dropping your
stride foot back, while turning your
lead shoulder with it. Catch the ball,
pick up your target, stride, and throw
to the base. On a cutoff, always throw
the ball overhand to the base. This
throw is much more accurate and
straightforward, making it easier to
catch. Figure 23 shows a player
positioned to throw the relay.

Figure 23

Practice Drills

WALL BALL DRILL

This is a simple drill that doesn't require any assistance.
Find a wall with fifteen to twenty feet of clearance. Place a
base or a similar object fifteen feet from the wall. Throw the
ball low against the wall, making the play on the "grounder"
simulated by the rebound. Another version of this drill is to
catch simulated throws from the infield. Instead of throwing
the ball low on the wall to create grounders, throw the ball
head-high and practice pivoting on the bag to catch the
rebound. A real baseball is not necessary here; a bouncing
ball actually works better (see Diagram 9).

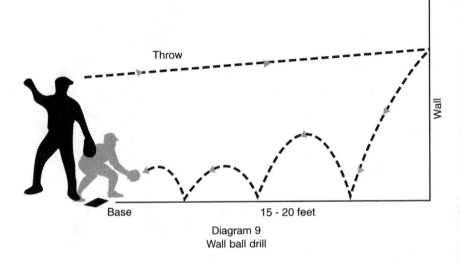

Diagram 9
Wall ball drill

As stated earlier, first base is an offensive position. Being a solid fielder is an advantage, but hitting is where you will win your position. Be sure to practice the mechanics covered here, but concentrate on swinging the bat. This is where your career will rise or fall.

Playing Middle Infield

The Warm-Up

Middle infielders depend on quickness and agility to cover the position they play. This position cannot be played with any type of leg or back injury. Therefore, you must pay special attention to stretching those areas. This or a similar routine will help you loosen up before the game.

1. Take a light jog around the field to warm your body and stretch your legs. Try to kick your knees high to enhance the muscle stretch.

2. Do groin and hamstring stretches, as well as quadriceps work. Give extra time and attention to these stretches.

3. Do trunk twists to stretch the back and sides. Sit on the ground and bring your legs back over your head. This is an outstanding stretch for your back.

4. Perform plenty of wind sprints. Some positions will wind sprint, but none more than the middle infield.

5. Play some toss, finishing with long toss. Your position will require a long throw at times, so be fully loose. During the toss, pay particular attention to your footwork.

Now that you have finished these exercises, you are ready for the infield.

Playing Middle Infield

Middle infielders—the shortstop and the second baseman—play two of the most active positions on the field. They may not have balls hit to them on every play, but they have a job on every pitch. They may have to back up a throw, direct the outfield, make a play on the hit, or throw the ball.

The shortstop and second baseman are a team. Each needs to know exactly where the other is at all times. For this reason we will cover these positions together.

FIELDING GROUNDERS

Unlike the first baseman—who can simply knock down the ball in an emergency and still have time to make the out at first base—middle infielders must consistently be able to field ground balls cleanly in order to make split-second plays.

The first move in fielding the ball is to stay low, with your knees bent. Bent knees and charging the ball are vital actions to making the play. If you attempt to catch the grounder while standing on the heels of your feet, the ball is likely to get an additional bounce, causing you to field it under your body where you may easily lose sight of it. Figure 24 shows the stance to be used as the ball is in flight from the pitcher to the plate. Notice how the player is creeping toward the plate with feet shoulder-width apart and knees bent. This enables him to make last-minute adjustments on a ball taking a bad hop. In addition, this stance will help him receive the ball one hop sooner—generally an easier play. When you have charged the ball and have decided the point at which to receive it, lower your butt and spread your feet to get nearer to the ground. Extend your arms forward, putting your glove well out in front of your body and making it clearly visible to you. Not extending your arms and leaving the glove between your legs makes it impossible for you to see the ball in relationship to the glove. This typically results in the ball hitting the heel of the glove or missing the glove altogether. Younger or inexperienced players are sometimes slow to react to grounders or freeze in place. The key is to be bold and keep moving!

Proper fielding mechanics are performed in Figures 25 and 26. This player is positioned low to the ground with a wide stance. His arms are extended to receive the ball and his weight is on his toes.

As the ball nears the glove, start to move the glove toward the ball in a scooping motion. If you leave the glove stationary, the hands are more rigid, increasing the chance that the ball will bounce out of your glove.

Figure 25

Figure 26

Figure 24

THROWING TO BASES

Once you've fielded the ground ball, set your feet, point your front shoulder toward the target, take a stride forward, and throw. On most plays there is no reason to rush. If you charged the ball and caught it cleanly, there is plenty of time to make the throw. If possible, throw the ball overhand. The overhand throw has less "tail" and is much more accurate. (see Figure 27).

One habit young players have is lobbing the ball across the field. A soft throw often results in an error. It is very hard to judge the distance the ball will cover when tossed lightly. Throw the ball firmly, making sure it will carry across the infield to its destination. Another problem with the lob is the pressure it puts on the player *catching* the ball. The runner has more time to run on the soft throw, making an infielder anxious about catching the ball. This can also result in errors.

Figure 27

BACKHAND PLAYS

The backhand play is a major part of the game for the shortstop and second baseman. Sometimes a middle infielder has to backhand the ball because it is impossible to catch it otherwise. In this situation, a short, quick movement toward the ball is desirable. The ball should be received in front of your body, just like the ball hit directly to you. The only real difference between this play and the others is the position of your body. As you approach the area to receive the ball, take one additional step with your left foot, turning your body sideways to the ball. Figure 28 shows proper form for the backhand.

Catch the ball forward of your front knee, slightly pushing the glove toward the ball. This will allow your body to pop up from the fielding position faster to make the throw. Also, should the ball hit the heel of the glove, it will bounce forward and remain in front of you.

DOUBLE PLAYS

This is where both the second baseman and the shortstop need to spend a lot of time practicing together. The double play is very difficult to accomplish without quickness and accuracy. The most important part of turning the double play is to first catch the grounder. Do not try to get ahead of yourself and do too much too fast. After successfully catching the ball, transfer the ball to your bare hand. From here, there are many different situations that can occur.

Figure 28

SITUATIONS FOR SHORTSTOPS:

1. When you're close to the bag, no stride is necessary. Pivot your hips toward second base and give the ball an

underhand toss. Be sure to make the ball visible early so the second baseman can see the throw in progress.

2. A medium-distance play requires a sidearm toss with no stride. After catching the ball pivot your hips toward second base, stay low to the ground, and give the ball a sidearm toss from the hip. Throwing from the right knee is acceptable if needed (see Figure 29).

3. The long play can be very tough. The combination of your long toss and the throw to first takes time. A sidearm throw is often needed on this play, just as it was needed in the medium-distance play. The only difference is that you will drop to the knee. You should not, however, throw from your knee. Throwing at ground level will limit the velocity generated on the throw. Stay on your feet and use the turn of your hips to add speed to your throw. All of these situations require you to open your front foot toward the bag to help clear your hips. A belt-high throw is desirable for all three plays because any other throw is harder to catch.

Figure 29

SITUATIONS FOR SECOND BASEMEN

1. When you're close to the bag use the underhand shovel toss. Do this by turning your upper body toward second base and underhanding the ball to the shortstop quickly with a "push" action. No stride is necessary here.

2. The medium-distance play also uses a sidearm throw, much like the shortstop's, but the footwork is much different. Here, dropping to one knee is almost always required. First, open your hips and drop to your right knee. Use a sidearm toss to throw the ball to second. An overhand throw, whenever possible, is even better because it is generally more accurate. (see Figure 30).

Figure 30

3. The long play is the most difficult play of all—even harder than the shortstop's long play. Here, you can use either the overhand or sidearm throw. If possible, try to stay on your feet because you will need the leverage to get velocity on the throw. After catching the ball, pivot your hips toward the bag and throw the ball with your weight on the back foot. If the double play is too hard, simply make the play at first base for one out.

THE PIVOT

The proper footwork around the bag can speed up a double play tremendously; slow footwork will reduce the chances of getting out the runner at first base. The mechanics of double-play footwork vary according to a player's position.

Shortstop: There are three ways to catch the ball and clear the bag to make the throw on to first. No matter which technique you use, time the play so you are not at the bag before the ball. If you get to the bag too early, your motion has stopped and a bad throw will pull you off the bag in pursuit of the ball, causing the runners to be safe at all bases.

In a play where the runner from first is not near the bag, the best move is to come across the bag, catch the ball and throw to first. No real footwork is required other than making sure you tag the base, take a stride toward first, and throw. The second type of move around the bag is a little tougher. As you approach the bag, catch the ball, tag the bag, sidestep toward right field, and throw to first base. This move will allow you to clear the runner, lessening the chance of your being "taken out" by a collision.

The third play is basically the same as the second, except that instead of clearing the bag toward right field, clear the bag in the direction of third base. Again, this is to allow you to make a throw around the runner. On a play where the runner is bearing down on you at second, catch the throw and jump over the runner sliding toward you. Figure 31 shows what can occur when the player does not clear the runner after the throw.

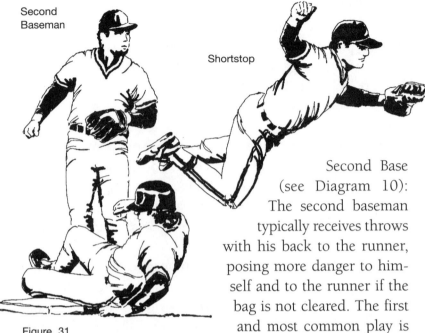

Second
Baseman

Shortstop

Figure 31

Second Base (see Diagram 10): The second baseman typically receives throws with his back to the runner, posing more danger to himself and to the runner if the bag is not cleared. The first and most common play is to catch the ball with the right foot on the bag, tag the base, take a short step with your right foot toward third base (while pivoting on your left), and throw to first (A). Use this play when the runner is a good distance from second base with no chance taking you out.

The second play is to catch the ball with your left foot on the bag, step off the bag toward right field with your left foot (while pivoting on your right), and throw to first (C).

The third and final play is to catch the ball with the left foot on the bag, stride with your right foot toward left field (while pivoting on your left) and throw from behind second base to first (B).

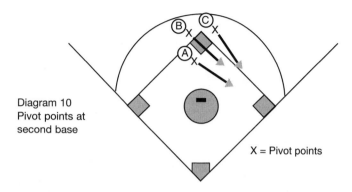

Diagram 10
Pivot points at
second base

X = Pivot points

POP-UPS

With good communication, these plays are not that difficult. Unlike every other position, the middle infielders have a clear view of the five players able to call for a pop-up. A rule of thumb to minimize confusion is: *the shortstop is in control of all pop-ups unless the outfielder calls him off.* There are rules as to who is in charge of the ball, but no matter what, the shortstop should be the decision-maker on infield flies. There are not a lot of coaching tips on the mechanics of catching pop-ups. The most important rule is: *keep your eye on the ball.* The other key to catching pop-ups is to keep your feet moving. Run hard until you have judged the ball, then slow down, being careful not to stop. If the ball is misjudged—or the wind blows or shifts—adjusting your position is much easier if your momentum is continuous.

BACKING UP THROWS

A little but important play that is often overlooked is backing up the throws. If there is a runner on base, especially third, the second baseman as well as the shortstop should

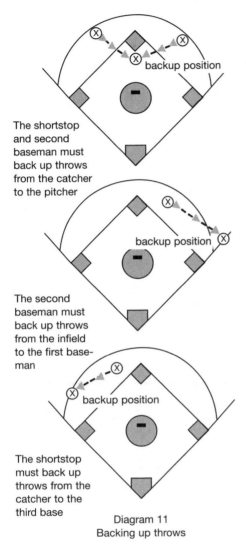

The shortstop and second baseman must back up throws from the catcher to the pitcher

The second baseman must back up throws from the infield to the first baseman

The shortstop must back up throws from the catcher to the third base

Diagram 11
Backing up throws

glide in behind the mound on all throws to the pitcher. If a ball is overthrown by the catcher to the pitcher, the runner on third could easily score. Also, the shortstop should back up the catcher's throws to third base to keep the runner from scoring on an overthrow. The second baseman should back up first base on all infield throws if he has no other responsibility on the play. Diagram 11 shows backup positions for throws.

COVERING STEALS

Proper positioning for throws is important if you plan on successfully throwing runners out. Communication between the shortstop and second baseman is also needed. With a runner on first, the middle infielders need to decide who will cover second base on each play. If communication is broken, both players will run to the base on a steal, causing a traffic jam at the bag.

After each pitch, the two players should look at each other. The shortstop is in charge and will decide who will cover the bag. He will open his mouth wide if he will cover the base. If his mouth is closed, the second baseman will cover. An easy way to remember this is: mouth open is "I," mouth closed is "you."

Now that you have decided who is covering the base, proper mechanics for the tag are needed. Run hard to the bag, standing just in front of the base. Provide a good target to the catcher. Stay low to the ground with bent knees. Do not catch the ball in front of the bag. Instead, let the ball travel all the way to the bag. It takes much longer for you to carry the ball to the bag than for the throw to reach it. Figure 32 shows the proper position for receiving the throw.

It's important to remember that the infielder who is not receiving the throw needs to back up the play. The proper position for the backup is on the outfield grass behind second base.

Make sure you keep the outfielders in the game. Every out that is recorded should be relayed to the outfield by the shortstop and the second baseman. Yell the number of outs as well as use your hand to signal them.

Figure 32

CUTOFFS

The final job of the middle infielders is to receive the balls thrown to the infield from the outfielders. On balls hit to the left or center fielder, the shortstop is the cutoff man. He should run halfway into the outfield—raising his arms high for visibility—and align himself with the bag. The player covering the base to receive the ball should assist in positioning him. Balls hit to right field are cut off by the second baseman, who should follow the same routine as the shortstop. The exceptions to this cutoff plan are balls hit to right field and thrown to third base, in which case both players will cut off; and balls hit to right field and thrown home, in which case the first baseman is the cutoff man.

The second baseman should be in the outfield grass and the shortstop should be near second base, ready to cover the bag if needed, or to catch the cutoff if it is overthrown to the second baseman. There is a proper way to receive and throw the cutoff that will greatly speed up the toss to the base. The first move is to drop your left foot back as the ball is in flight. This will enable you to pick up the target (the next player to receive the ball) faster. The next move is to catch the ball beside your body while taking a stride toward the target. Align your shoulders with the base to which you are throwing and fire a belt-high throw. If the distance is too great to cover in the air, "long hop" the ball to the bag (throw the ball so that it bounces far enough in front of the baseman for him to catch it waist-high). Do not "short hop" the baseman. It is much easier to catch the ball on a long or second hop. Figure 33 shows the cutoff man "squaring-up" or aligning his feet and body in the proper position to throw to the target before releasing the ball.

These are the most common techniques used in middle infielding.
Quick feet and sure hands are key to
becoming a solid fielder. Remember,
you will receive more fielding chances than
anyone on the field.

Practice Drills

DRY DRILLS

Standing on the field at second base, run
through the double-play techniques. Practice
both the throw to the second base bag, and
receiving the ball and throwing it to first. Pay
special attention to the position of your feet
and body throughout the play.

FRONT-END DRILL

Instead of having three players
available to turn the double play, you only need

Figure 33

two. Have someone stand on second base while you field
balls. As you catch each ball, pivot and make a belt-high
throw to second base. This drill will help you to practice the
throw and the footwork necessary to complete the double
play.

BACK-END DRILL

This drill is similar to the front-end drill. The only difference is that instead of catching grounders, you will receive
the throws. Start by standing a few feet from the bag. As the
other player starts to throw, rush the bag and receive the ball.

It is not necessary to proceed to throw to first; just work on the speedy transfer of the ball to your bare hand.

All drills are great, but the best drill of all is fielding grounders. Take as many grounders as possible. While catching the ground balls, work really hard on the mechanics. A shortstop has to be the best fielder on the diamond, followed by the second baseman. Fielding extra ground balls should be a daily part of your pre-game routine. There is no substitute for practice.

6

Third Base

The Warm-Up

Third base requires quick reactions. The range of motion needed to play effectively here is four or five steps in any direction. For this reason, the most important body parts to warm up are the legs and the arms. Loose legs will enable you to perform short, fast movements to make the plays at the "hot corner." After receiving the ball, you will have to throw it across the field. This means your throwing arm must be completely loose. Here are some helpful exercises to prepare your body.

1. As with every other position, start with a jog around the field to warm up your body and loosen your legs.

2. A good regimen of leg stretches is important at this point. Do some hamstring, groin, and quad stretches.

3. Do trunk twists to loosen the back and sides. Sitting on the ground and lifting your legs over your head is a great way to loosen your back.

4. Shoulder shrugs and arm circles are good exercises to warm the arms. Some triceps stretches will also help.

5. Do some wind sprints to finish warming up your body before playing toss.

6. Now that you are loose, play toss. Finish your pre-game warm-up with some quick long toss as detailed on page 25. This practice will come in handy on those long throws across the infield.

Playing Third Base

The third base position is much like being a hockey goalie. Your job is to knock down all the hot shots to prevent doubles. Unlike the middle infield positions, you must use your body to keep balls in the infield—and hopefully recover to throw the runner out. In Figure 34, the player is in position to stop balls hit at him. Notice how his feet are spread, his knees are bent, and his stance is low-to-the-ground. From this position the third baseman will be expected to move four or five steps in any direction to field the ball.

Figure 34

As the ball is hit, get on your toes in front of the ball. You need to knock the ball down if you can't glove it—whereas the middle infielders are trying to catch the ball cleanly. The third baseman has a shorter throw to make than the shortstop so he can afford, if necessary, to stop the ball and then pick it up. The next move is to set your feet, align your right shoulder with the target, take a stride, and throw to first. It is important to try to throw overhand. A sidearm or underhand throw is likely to result in extra errors because these throws are harder to control. Try to make all your throws to first base chest-high, thereby making them easier to catch. Figure 35 shows a sidearm throw, which is *not* recommended.

Figure 35

BACKHAND PLAYS

Another play that will be used extensively at third base is the backhand play. Many balls will be hit to the right of the third baseman with enough velocity that he will be unable to knock them down with his body. Here, if the backhand play is not used, a double is almost guaranteed. The first move in attempting the backhand play is a crossover step. The left leg must cross in front of your body as you bring your glove hand toward the baseline. The glove should be below your head, in front of your body, and slightly tilted (Figure 36 shows perfect positioning for the backhand play). A "tilt" to the glove means the tip of the webbing should be forward of the heel of the glove. This will help keep the ball in the glove on a hard shot. If the tip of the webbing is behind the heel, the ball will tumble out, making it impossible to finish the play.

Occasionally, you will need to leap and dive to make this play. Try to keep the glove in the tilted position, if possible. When you have fielded the ball, reset your feet, point your shoulder toward the target, and throw the ball firmly across the infield. Be sure to stride toward the target. Throwing the ball from third base with no stride will

Figure 36

reduce your velocity, often resulting in an undesirable short hop at first base. Figure 37 pictures a third base-man striding and throwing to first base.

Bunt Fielding

Another play that often affects the third base position is the swinging bunt. You will need to field this ball barehand-ed and throw off balance. The first move on this play is to rush the ball quickly using short, choppy steps. If you run toward the ball with long strides, it will be very difficult to catch the ball on your left foot. Large strides will also make adjustments hard, because a ball can easily catch you in mid-stride. Stay low to the ground with bent knees. Pick up the ball with your bare hand while landing on your left foot. As soon as the ball is picked up, take one more stride with your right foot and unload the ball—even though you may be off balance—toward first base. If for some reason you do not have a good grip on the ball, be sure to throw low, giving the first baseman a chance to catch the ball. A high throw will fly into right field, giving an additional base to the runner.

Figure 37

Even though this play is made on the run, balance is important. At the point of release, your right leg should be directly under your body and provide enough balance to make an accurate throw. Although throwing overhand is normally recommended, this play is best completed with a sidearm toss from the hip. Figure 38 shows the bare-hand play using a sidearm toss.

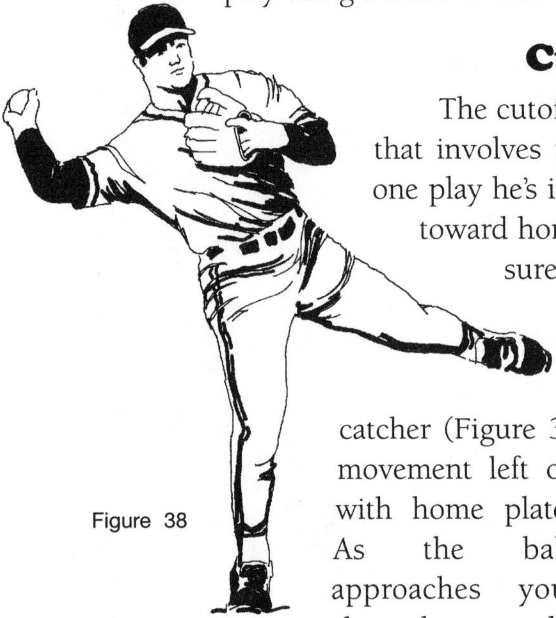

Cutoffs

The cutoff is another type of play that involves the third baseman. The one play he's in charge of is the throw toward home by the left fielder. Be sure to hustle to the cutoff spot, raise your arms high, and listen for instructions from the catcher (Figure 39). He will direct your movement left or right, and align you with home plate. As the ball approaches your glove, drop your left foot backward to open your hips, catch the ball, stride toward the target, and make a belt-high throw to the catcher. Diagram 12 shows cutoff spots for various positions and plays.

Figure 38

Double Plays

Double plays are simple to perform from third base. Just remember that the ball must travel all the way around the infield so it's up to you to make an easy-to-catch

Figure 39

throw to the second baseman. Try to throw overhand, but keep in mind that the ball fielded to your left will probably require a sidearm toss.

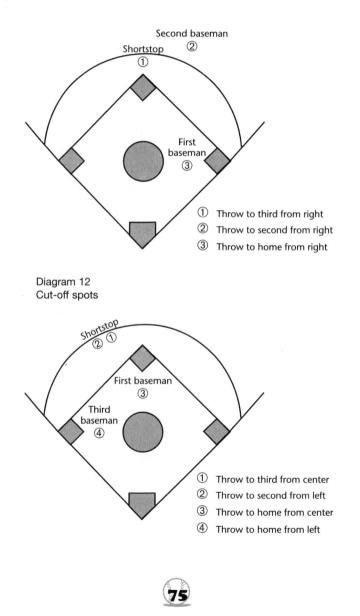

Diagram 12
Cut-off spots

① Throw to third from right
② Throw to second from right
③ Throw to home from right

① Throw to third from center
② Throw to second from left
③ Throw to home from center
④ Throw to home from left

Regardless of who calls the ball, all grounders hit to your left that you are capable of fielding are your responsibility. It is much easier for you to catch this ground ball and make the throw than it is for the shortstop. He will need more time to field the ball and will have to make a longer throw, giving the runner extra time to beat the ball.

Third base is a fun position to play. You will have a variety of balls to field. There is more emphasis on instant reaction here than at any other position on the field. Unfortunately, there are very few practice drills to help you improve. The best way to master your skills is to field as many ground balls as possible. Be sure to focus on your mechanics when catching all practice grounders. Good practice habits turn into good game habits.

7

Outfield Play

The Warm-Up

The most important body parts used in the outfield are the legs. Outfielders are required to track down many balls—sometimes a great distance. There are not as many balls hit to your position as there are to others, but a good outfielder has a place to run to on every play.

The other body part used here is the arm. For instance, you may be asked to throw a ball as far as you can to get the game-winning run out at the plate. Here are some pre-game stretches to prepare you for the game.

1. Run a lap around the field, kicking your knees high. Vary your speed to warm the body and loosen the legs.

2. Spend a lot of time stretching the hamstrings and quads, two very important muscles in your position.

3. Do some groin stretches. A pulled groin could sideline you for a long time.

4. Do arm circles, triceps stretches, and shoulder shrugs to loosen the arms.

5. Be sure to do plenty of wind sprints to completely loosen your legs. Your position will require you to sprint from spot to spot throughout the game.

6. Play toss, finishing with plenty of long toss. This will be your primary throw during the game.

Now you are ready for the infield-outfield practice. Between innings the center fielder should bring a ball for the outfielders to toss so that they stay loose. While playing toss between innings, continue to stretch your legs. The late innings are hours from your initial warm-up. Meanwhile, the legs can stiffen.

Communication

It's vital to remember that there are three outfielders and four infielders playing defense. On a fly ball, nobody is glancing at the other players. All attention is focused skyward. This makes it very important to call for the ball. Keep in mind that there are rules covering who is in charge of the play: The center fielder is in control of all balls, in the infield or the outfield, if he can get to them. The other outfielders are in charge of all flies the center fielder cannot reach. The left and right fielders can call off all infielders on a fly ball. Injuries can easily occur when players are running full-speed and looking upward. The proper call when taking charge of a fly is, " I got it." Repeat this call loudly, two or three times. Remain quiet if you cannot get to the ball so as not to create confusion, and stay clear of the player who called the ball. A player hearing footsteps nearby may take his eye off the ball, causing an error. If you see another player running in the direction of the player catching the ball, try to hold him back to avoid a collision. Figure 40 shows poor communication.

Playing the Outfield

FOOTWORK

The most important part of getting to fly balls is footwork. Poor movement at the crack of the bat accounts for most misplayed balls.

It is much harder to move backward on a fly ball than forward, so your first movement on all hits balls should be a drop-step back. At that point, you can easily continue backward or, if the ball is short of your position, you can easily change direction and move forward. If your first move is for-

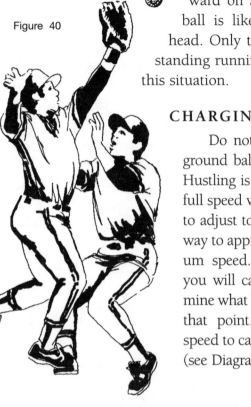

Figure 40

ward on a fly ball hit deep, the ball is likely to drop over your head. Only the outfielder with outstanding running speed can overcome this situation.

CHARGING BALLS

Do not run full speed toward ground balls hit in your direction. Hustling is important, but running full speed will make it very difficult to adjust to a bad hop. The proper way to approach the ball is at medium speed. Decide at what point you will catch the ball and determine what kind of hop will occur at that point. Adjust your running speed to catch the ball on a big hop (see Diagrams 13 and 14).

Diagram 13 - Incorrect point to field the ball

Diagram 14 - Proper point to field the ball

GET THE ANGLE

A player with great speed does not have to worry about the angle he takes to reach the ball—although if he can get the correct angle, he can cover even more ground. As with all outfield plays, judging the course and speed of the ball is the first step. Unfortunately, this cannot be taught, but as a rule of thumb, the angle you take in pursuit of the ball should be as direct a line as possible to the point where you judge the ball can be caught. Diagram 15 points out some of the most common angles to be taken—or avoided.

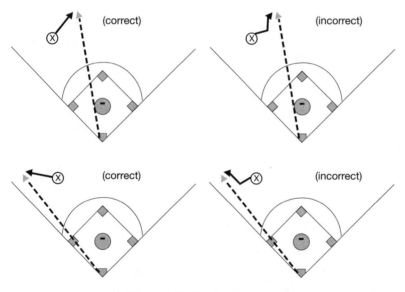

Diagram 15 - Getting the angle

BACKING UP

It bears repeating that the outfielders have a place to be on every play. While there are not as many balls hit directly to outfield positions, that doesn't mean you should just stand afield and watch the game. Diagram 16 shows where outfielders should position themselves to play back-up on ground balls. Make sure that when the play calls for you to provide backup, you run full-speed to the required spot.

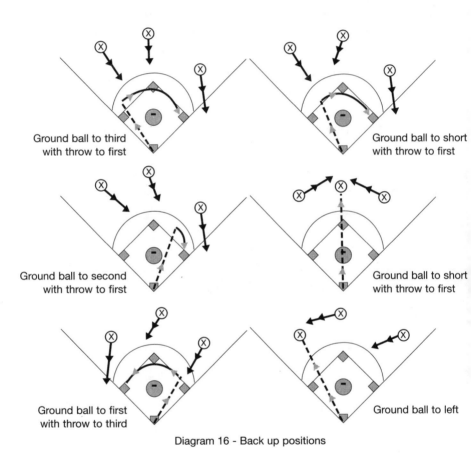

Ground ball to third
with throw to first

Ground ball to short
with throw to first

Ground ball to second
with throw to first

Ground ball to short
with throw to first

Ground ball to first
with throw to third

Ground ball to left

Diagram 16 - Back up positions

THROWING

It would be ideal if every outfielder had an outstanding throwing arm. Unfortunately, most outfielders do not. Regardless of your arm strength, a cutoff man is needed. Therefore, when throwing balls to the infield, you should always target the cutoff man. Even if you have enough arm strength to throw the ball all the way, the ball should be thrown low enough to allow a cutoff man to intercept it should it need to go to a different base than initially thought.

Whenever you throw the ball, make sure your feet are planted on the ground and you have good balance. Point your front shoulder toward the target and make the throw. It may seem more efficient to simply get the ball and give it a heave, but the probable inaccuracy of and lack of speed on the ball is likely to cost both time and bases.

Decide before the play unfolds what you plan to do with the ball if it is hit to you. Don't wait until the ball is in your glove to figure out where it goes. A good rule of thumb is to try to get the ball to the cutoff man as soon a possible and let him worry about where it goes. The cutoff man is an infielder who deals with base runners much more than you do. When throwing to the cutoff man, do not short-hop your throw to him. If he is too far for you to reach, long-hop him. He will easily be able to make this play and relay the ball to the base.

A skillful outfielder can save his team many runs in the course of the season. Learn the mechanics of good defense and you will be just as productive to your team defensively as you are offensively. Next, some practice drills to help your defense.

Practice Drills

TENNIS RACKET FLIES

This is one of the best drills to teach the footwork required for fly balls. You'll need a tennis racket, some wiffle balls, and one more person. Have the other player stand twenty-five to thirty feet in front of you with the tennis racket. Get in the playing position and field the wiffle balls he hits over your head or to your side. Tennis racket flies can be placed with greater accuracy than those produced with a bat from home plate; you'll have to quicken your reaction time and practice proper footwork to catch them.

LONG TOSS

This drill was mentioned in chapter 2 as a way to loosen the throwing arm, but it is also an outstanding way to build arm strength. It is not important to throw the ball on line to the other player—just throw the ball as far as possible. Before progressing to maximum-distance throws, be sure that you are completely loose so as to avoid injury.

LIVE BALLS

As with every other position on the field, there is no substitute for live fly balls off the bat. Whenever possible, take as many fly balls and grounders as you can. The more practice you have, the better you'll become.

Defense is only half of your job as an outfielder. Do not neglect the offensive part of the game. Many major league outfielders are not there for their defense. They are playing at the major league level because they can really swing the bat!

8

Base Running
&
Base Coaching

Base Running

There are many different situations that can arise while circling the bases. We do not have enough time to cover every play that may occur, but we can cover the ones you're most likely to encounter. No matter what the situation, be sure to watch the base coach. His job is to direct the runners around the bases. Something that cannot be base-coached, however, is hustle. Be sure to be an aggressive baserunner, regardless of the situation.

INFIELD GROUNDER

The proper strategy when running out the infield grounder is to run "through" the bag. Run full-blast down the base line, not slowing until you have "run through" (past) the first-base bag by at least fifteen feet. Do not slow down unless directed to do so by the base coach. Be sure to tag the very center of the bag. When you touch the base on its side, you run the risk of turning your ankle. There is a restraining area which should be used as your path to first base if the ball is hit near home plate and the catcher is throwing the ball. If the thrown ball hits you outside the restraining area you are out. Diagram 17 shows the restraining area adjacent to the first base line.

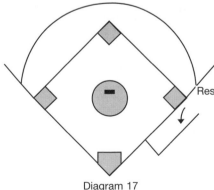

Restraining area

Diagram 17
First base restraining area

BASE HIT

Make sure the ball is through the infield and

you've checked with the base coach before running the bases in this manner. On a base hit, round the bag to help you see the field and judge whether to take the extra base on a misplayed ball. "Round the bag" by running hard to the start of the restraining line. At this point, break right toward the coach's box and then left across the bag, facing second base. With this style of base running be sure to overrun the bag to some extent, but retain enough control to return to the bag—or take second base, if possible. Diagram 18 sketches the route on the base hit.

EXTRA BASES

This style of base running is much like running out the base hit, except you will proceed to run to second. If you hit a double and there is no chance to advance, or if the ball is being thrown to second to make a play on you, do not

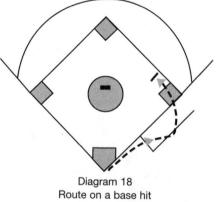

Diagram 18
Route on a base hit

leave the bag. The best way to stay on the bag is to slide (a technique covered later in this chapter). If the hit has a chance of being a triple, round second base and "pick up"—that is, glance at—the base coach. He may wave you on to third. As you approach third, confirm with the base coach again. If he is satisfied with third, stay on or near the bag. If the base coach calls you to take another base, continue rounding third and head for home. Diagram 19 illustrates how to round the bases.

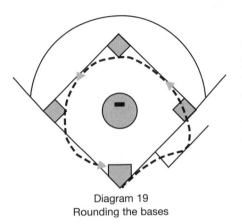

Diagram 19
Rounding the bases

Notice that the lines on Diagram 19 touch the inside of the bases. Touching the inside of the bases is faster and helps you to change direction toward the next base. Touching the top of the base can easily cause you to slip and fall. Some coaches will try to teach you to touch all the bases with the left foot. This is correct, but if it causes you to change or slow your stride, it's not worth it. The most important thing is to run hard and touch all the bases cleanly.

SLIDING

Sliding is one of the most important base-running techniques. Sliding can also include a head-first slide. A head-first slide is not recommended, however, as it is very dangerous. Your hand, wrist, or fingers can easily be injured. Therefore, this slide will not be covered here.

As you head toward the base on a hit, the first move in attempting a slide is to jump off your right foot into the air.

Figure 41
The slide

Do not slow down to perform a slide—maintain your running speed.

While in the air, bend your right knee under your body and extend the left leg. As your body approaches the ground, raise your hands upward so they are not caught under your body. As the left foot touches the base, lean forward; this will cause you to pop upright, ready to continue to the next base, if possible. The slide play should begin well before the base, though an exact distance cannot be specified. The distance depends upon the speed of the runner and the hardness of the ground. Figure 41 depicts a proper slide.

Base running is much like every other aspect of baseball. You will have to practice to improve. Running speed is a real advantage, especially when trying to steal a base. We will not cover base stealing in this handbook, however, because at this level, stealing is not very complicated.

Remember, when running the bases, always watch the base coach.

BASE COACH SIGNALS TO THE HITTER AND THE RUNNER

The two most common signals used by the base coach are arm circles, which call for you to continue running, and arms held straight up in the air, which means to hold at the base you're on. Watching the base coaches instead of the ball will keep you from losing speed—and being thrown out on a close play.

The third base coach almost always gives the signals to the hitter. These signals instruct the hitter as to whether he should swing, not swing, or bunt; and instruct the runner as to whether he should steal a base.

Coaches should signal their players (and hitters and runners should look for their signal) prior to the hitter stepping up to the plate. The hitter should glance at the third base coach for instruction while the runner should remain on base until the signal is given. If a runner steps off the base, he may not be well enough informed to avoid being tagged out.

Signals are not given during time-outs. Generally, they are given during the course of the game. A signal could be as simple as a touch of the hat or a clap of the hands. Before the game, the base coach or manager should have a meeting to explain what the signals are so that every player is familiar with the calls. At the lower levels of play, signals are usually designed to be easy to remember: a touch of the shirt is the sign to steal (both begin with the letter "S"), a touch of the belt is the sign to bunt (both begin with the letter "B") and so on. Sometimes an "indicator" is used. An indicator is simply an alert that the *next touch* signifies the play being called. For example, a coach will tell his team that the indicator is a touch of his face. Any touch that immediately follows the indicator is the signal.

Another common signal that is designated before the game begins is "take off" which, in effect, erases whatever signal the base coach has just communicated because it is wrong, or because he wants to start the signal or signals over. An example of a take-off signal is a swipe of the leg. The advantage of designating a take off is that the coach does not need to call a time-out in order to clarify or cancel his signals.

The final sign you'll need to know is the "finish." It is very important for the hitter and the runner to know when the coach is finished signaling. A very easy signal for the finish is a clap of the hands or a coach's slight turn away from the hitter.

Base coaching may seem inconsequential, but many games are won or lost by the base coach's instructions. When runners are running the bases, they can't see where the ball is or who is throwing it. In essence, the base coach becomes the eyes and ears of the runner.

Runners sometimes lose track of the outs as well as who's on base, so the base coach also keeps runners aware of this vital information.

9

Hitting

Up to this point, we have discussed defense. Another part of baseball that is equally as important is *offense*. There are many players in the major leagues that are strictly offensive players. Being a good hitter will almost guarantee you a spot in the lineup no matter how poor a fielder you may be. The following pages will explain the mechanics of hitting. Keep in mind that not every player is the same or has the same ability. What works for one person may not necessarily work for another. These mechanics are guidelines for becoming a better hitter. If they do not seem to work for you, master the style of hitting with which you feel most comfortable.

Mechanics

THE STANCE

The stance is the way you stand in the box awaiting the pitch. This is probably the most variable of all the mechanics. It really doesn't matter how you stand at the plate, as long as you feel comfortable and can quicky spot the ball as it leaves the pitcher's hand.

The following figures display common stances. Notice that the players—regardless of the position of their bat—are well balanced with their bodies centered over their legs. The distance between your feet doesn't matter as long as your stride is under control as you attack the ball.

Figure 42 shows a flat-bat stance, while Figure 43 shows a tall-bat stance. Although bat position doesn't make a difference, notice that both players place their hands in a similar position. Now, let's break down the swing, beginning with the most basic and important rule: No matter what type of swing you use, *keep your eye on the ball!* The sooner a hitter can spot or "pick up" the ball and follow it, the better. Try to find the ball in the pitcher's hand and then follow it to the bat.

The first move when attempting to hit the ball is to stride. Do this by picking up the front foot and charging it toward the ball. As a general rule, the stride (shown in Figure 44) should be half the distance of your stance. If you are having problems catching up to the ball with your swing, your stride should be shortened so that you can swing the bat into the strike zone faster. Notice how the hitter slightly lifts his front leg as he strides. On television you may see some players lift their front leg high off the ground. These players are very strong and have mastered the

Figure 42
Flat-bat stance

Figure 43
Tall-bat stance

Figure 44
The stride

hitting technique. For younger players, a small, quick stride is recommended.

Figure 45
The trigger

The next job is to get the bat moving. Do this by starting the hands—the part of the swing known as the "trigger." Figure 45 shows the hands in motion. The most common preliminary or "trigger" movement is slightly back. This is very similar to winding up to hit the ball. The amount of hand movement depends upon how strong the player is and how fast the pitcher is throwing the ball. The hand movement should be adjusted according to these factors. A hand hitch—when the hands' first move is up or down—will slow the swing drastically, causing pop-ups or swings without contact.

Return your striding (front) foot to the ground. Now, you must get the bat into the strike zone. With your hands back and front foot on the ground, begin to shift your weight toward the pitcher with your back leg. During this process, drive your front elbow quickly toward the pitcher while pushing your top hand toward the front of the plate. This action will throw the barrel of the bat into contact position. As you start the swing, pivot your back foot in a spinning action, lifting the heel off the ground, as seen in Figure 46. Take special notice of how the process of pivoting the back foot has caused the back leg to form the letter "L," an indication that the rotation of the lower body has been performed correctly.

Figures 47 and 48 show how the bat has reached the plate with full extension. At this point in the swing the feet are firmly

Figure 46
The pivot

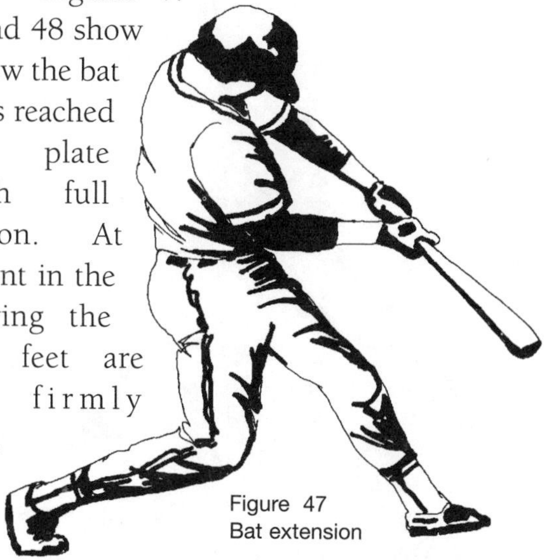

Figure 47
Bat extension

planted on the ground with the stride complete. The weight of the body is on the back leg, which is used as leverage to drive the ball. The body should be centered over the legs and the front foot slightly pointed inward. Be sure to keep your head "on" (turned toward) the ball. The best way to keep your head positioned properly is to keep your chin down and between your shoulders.

Figures 47 and 48 depict players keeping their head on the ball. In Figure 49, however, the player has taken his head off

Figure 48
Keeping your head
on the ball

the ball—causing a swing and a miss. Notice the huge difference in the positioning of the head.

At this point in the swing, only the "finish" remains. This is simple if you have done everything else correctly. Figures 50, 51, and 52 demonstrate the follow-through on the swing. Focus on getting extension to avoid cutting

Figure 49
Taking your head off the ball

Figure 51

Figure 50
The finish

Figure 52

the swing short; a fully extended swing will help to generate power and result in additional distance on the ball.

Common Problems

HAND HITCH

A hand hitch, shown in Figure 53, occurs when a hitter, in the process of swinging the bat, adds too much hand movement. The proper action is slightly back followed by an aggressive, forward swing at the ball. The hitter with a hand hitch will drop his hands down (toward his waist) instead of back as recommended. Any action other than slightly back is considered a hand hitch.

Figure 53
Hand hitch

"PULLING OFF THE BALL"

This problem occurs when a hitter does not attack the ball. The hitter will step toward the baseline instead toward the pitcher. This is normally referred to as "stepping in the bucket." Another way to pull off the ball is with the shoulders. In a proper swing, the front shoulder will drive toward the pitcher until the bat clears the strike zone. In an incorrect swing, the front shoulder rotates too early, leaving the chest of the hitter exposed to the

Figure 54
Pulling off
the ball

99

mound. Pulling off the ball makes it harder to reach the outside pitch. It also makes it harder to keep your eye on and make contact with the pitched ball because your head is moving away from the incoming pitch. Figure 54 shows a hitter pulling off the ball.

SWEEPING SWING

This occurs when a hitter's swing is too long. The simplest way to spot this problem is to look at the hitter's front arm. In a sweeping swing, the hitter will lock his front elbow causing his arm to stiffen in the straight-arm position. At this point, a hitter will find it virtually impossible to make split-second adjustments to hit the ball. In a correct swing, the arms are loose, bent at the elbows, and held close to the body until the contact point of the swing. Figure 55 shows a sweeping position.

Figure 55
Sweeping
swing
position

Practice Drills

SHADOW SWINGS

Every player ever to swing a bat has performed this drill. It can be a great learning tool if done correctly, but more often than not, players usually just go through the motions. To do this drill, set your feet as if you were in the batter's box. Imagine the pitch approaching the plate. Practice your footwork and swing, paying special attention to proper form.

(This drill is even more beneficial when it is performed in front of a mirror!)

SHORT TOSS DRILL

Short toss, which requires one additional player, is an outstanding drill designed to quicken your swing. Hopefully, a backstop is available but a net from the hitting cage is just as effective. Get into your stance with the bat in your hands. Have the other player kneel on one knee

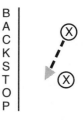

BACKSTOP

Diagram 20
Short toss drill

beside you and lightly toss the balls (underhand) knee-high in the strike zone for you to hit into the backstop. Diagram 20 indicates the players' proper position for this drill.

BATTING TEE DRILL

Almost every player has performed this drill. In fact, younger players typically use this batting aide to produce offense instead of using pitchers. It's important to remember that although the base of the tee serves as "home plate," home plate is not where the tee should be placed. The proper position of the tee is one foot *forward* of the plate. This is where actual contact is made.

On all drills, make sure to concentrate on your footwork and balance. Without these you will never become a good hitter. And remember, no matter how much time you spend on drills, there is no substitute for actual game swings.

Bunting

Unfortunately, none of the swing-related drills taught here cover bunting. This is a part of hitting which often is overlooked but is an important part of offense. Bunting can be used to advance runners, squeeze runs home, or, if learned well enough, to create base hits. The whole process of bunting depends on strikes. It is very hard to bunt a ball that is out of the strike zone. And as with every other part of the game, practice is essential.

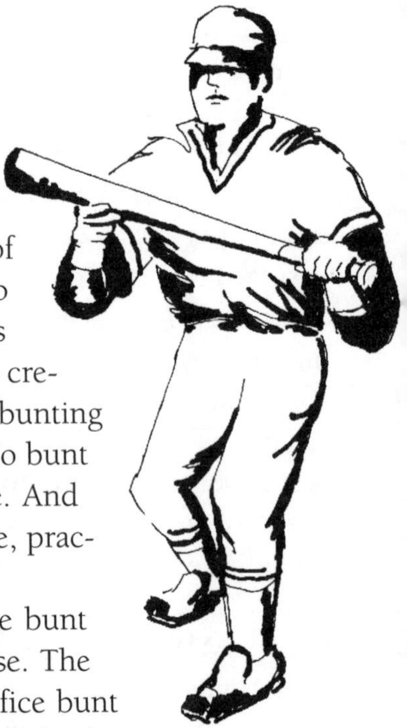

The sole purpose of a sacrifice bunt is to move a runner to the next base. The first move when attempting a sacrifice bunt is to position your body properly. Do this by pivoting your back foot toward the pitcher. Turn your back foot so that the toes are facing the mound. Now, slide your top hand up the bat, approximately to the label. The bottom hand should then slide to the top of the handle (see Figure 56). Also, a correct grip of the bat will find you wrapping your thumb around the bat with your top hand while the bottom hand holds the bat just as you would in a normal swing.

Figure 56
The bunt

The next move is to raise the head of the bat above the hands. This is done to help control the bat. The objective here is to catch the ball with the bat. Be sure to keep your head facing the ball and the bat in front of the plate. If you fail to extend the bat in front of the plate, the ball will be bunted foul. Be sure to square yourself to the pitcher early to set your body in position to bunt the ball (Figure 57 is an incorrect position for the bat to bunt).

Try to bunt the ball between the mound and the first base line. The best bunts are close to the line, but the sacrifice is considered successful if someone other than the pitcher fields the ball. Even if

Figure 57
Incorrect Bunting
Position

the pitcher does field the ball, the sacrifice can still be successful if the ball was not bunted directly to the pitcher.

The other type of bunt is a "drag bunt" which is used to attempt a base hit. This type of bunt is used by the player with excellent running speed. The first move is to drop the back foot instead of pivoting on it. This is done by stepping about one foot backward and six inches away from the plate. Next, slide your top hand up the bat while starting to move out of the batter's box. Make sure the head of the bat is in front of the strike zone to insure a fair ball. Unlike the sacrifice bunt, the grip on the top hand is not with just the thumb, but with the fingers wrapped fully around the bat. Be sure to grip the bat at the label just as you did on the sacrifice bunt. This manner of grip is used to help disguise the drag bunt from the fielders. Watch the ball make contact with the bat as you begin to run down the base line.

The previous instructions for the drag bunt were for a right-handed batter. The following directions are for the left-handed bunt. First, bring the back foot around toward the plate as the ball is in flight. As the ball approaches the strike zone, slide the hand up the bat (just as described in the right-handed drag bunt using an identical grip). Drop the head of the bat in front of the plate, making contact with the ball as you start your run up the base line. Do not look to see if the ball is fair or foul, just run full speed. Figure 58 shows a left-handed player bunting.

Don't give the bunt away by squaring too early. The proper time to pivot is when the pitcher's front leg hits the ground. Another thing to remember when attempting to bunt is to check the position of the infielders. Make sure they are playing deep. Otherwise, a bunt will make for an easy out.

The only real practice for the bunt can be done during batting practice. Be sure to take a few bunts while in the batter's box. There are no special bunt drills to help you acquire this skill. The only drill that might help you learn to bunt is "pepper." Pepper is played with as many players as you want. One player is the batter and the other players are fielders. The players stand in a line tossing the ball to the hitter. In turn, he swings or bunts the ball to the fielders. The player fielding the ball then throws to the hitter and so on. The defensive men stand fifteen to twenty feet from the hitter. When he hits a ball in the air and it's

Figure 58
The drag bunt

caught, his turn is finished and the player catching the ball is up to bat.

BATTING AVERAGES

The batting average is computed by dividing a player's number of hits by his number of times at bat. "At bats" is the number of times a hitter attempts to hit in a season excluding all walks, sacrifice flies, and sacrifice bunts.

For example, 30 hits in 100 at bats is calculated as follows: 30 – 100 = .300 batting average.

This statistic gauges the success of a hitter. Most major league hitters are considered "good" if they bat .280 or better. A .400 batting average has only been reached a handful of times in the history of major league baseball. Hitters with the best batting averages typically bat at the top of the lineup in the 1–4 positions.

10

Keeping
Score

Scoring is a very important part of the game. If a game is played without a scorekeeper, there will be no official record of the game's activity. At first glance, the score book will seem very confusing, but it is very easy to understand once you know the terms. The next few pages will explain scorekeeping terms and symbols, and how to use them properly.

The first thing you must remember when keeping score is that the scorekeeper is charged with recording all the activity taking place. Be sure to watch the entire play before attempting to mark anything in the official book. Often, scorers try to write during the play and end up missing some of the action.

Every player on the field is assigned a position number (which has no relationship to the uniform number). These position numbers correspond to the scorer's record of the ball's path during the course of a game. Diagram 21 and its accompanying chart show the standard number assigned to each position.

Before you learn to keep score, take some time to look at the score book. While some score books have the scoring terms printed in each box, we'll use a score sheet without preprinted terms so that you can learn how to score a game quickly and easily. Keep in mind that as you become a more experienced scorer, you'll devise your own scorekeeping system or routine, but for now, we'll keep it simple.

Below is an example of a score sheet. Notice that it has columns for the batting lineup, each player's position, and the innings. To avoid confusion later, be sure to list the batting order and positions correctly at the start of the game.

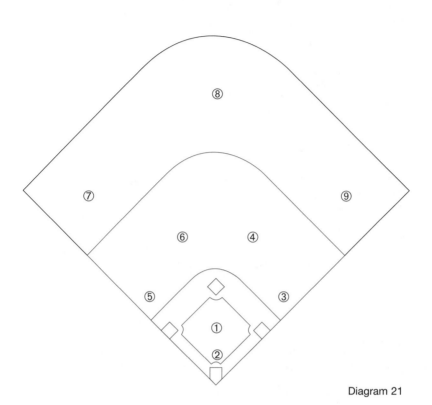

Diagram 21

POSITION CHART

1 - pitcher

2 - catcher

3 - first baseman

4 - second baseman

5 - third baseman

6 - shortstop

7 - left fielder

8 - center fielder

9 - right fielder

DH - designated hitter (hits in place of the pitcher)

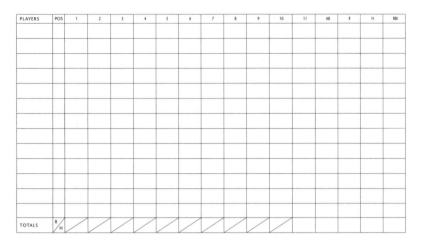

PLAYERS	POS	1	2	3	4	5	6	7	8	9	10	11	AB	R	H	RBI
TOTALS	R/H															

Diagram 22
Score sheet

Additional sites for recording information on the score sheet include:

AB - the total number of times a player was at bat

R - the total number of runs the player scored

H - the total number of hits the player made

RBI - the total number of runs the hitter drove (batted) in

R/H - the number of runs and hits made by all players in a single inning

Previously, we examined the position-number system used by the scorekeeper. Now, let's discuss how to use these numbers to record a game. Any legal play, and its result, must be recorded in the score book. Diagram 23 records the following plays:

PLAYER	POS	1	2
SMITH	5	6-3 ①	
WILSON	7	1B	

Diagram 23

In the first inning, player Smith hit a ground ball to the shortstop (in position 6), who threw the ball to first base (position 3) for an out. The circled "1" at the bottom of the box indicates that the first out of the inning was the result of the play. The scoring box is also used to record the base paths. Notice that the next player at bat, Wilson, hit a single (1B)—so a small, darkened square is drawn in the corner to indicate that Wilson reached first base.

Diagram 24, below, demonstrates how to record baserunning results.

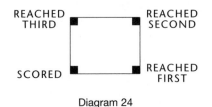

Diagram 24

Before we continue, review the list of symbols in Diagram 25, which are used to record possible activities and outcomes of a play:

SYMBOLS FOR SCORING

1B Single Base Hit	**2B** Double (2-base hit)
3B Triple (3-base hit)	**HR** Home Run
E Error	**BB** Walk, base on balls
IB Intentional Walk	**HP** Hit by Pitch
K Strikeout	**FC** Fielder's Choice
F Fly Ball Out	**DP** Double Play
SB Stolen Base	**CS** Caught Stealing
U Unassisted Play	**PO** Runner Picked Off Base
***R** Run Batted In	**WP** Wild Pitch
PB Passed Ball	**BK** Balk
SF Sacrifice Fly	**SH** Sacrifice Bunt

*Short for RBI in the interest of time and space on the score sheet

Diagram 25

There are a few rules of thumb you'll need to know to score a game properly.

For example, the "K" symbol is used when a player strikes out. If a hitter strikes out without swinging at strike three, however, a backward "K" is used. If a fly ball is caught, the "F" symbol is used and precedes the position number of the player that caught the ball. But if the fly ball was caught in foul territory, the "F" symbol follows the position number. Hence, a fly ball to left field is marked F-7 and a fly ball caught in foul territory is marked 7-F.

Another scoring symbol you'll need to be familiar with relates to the Unassisted Play. If a ball is hit and fielded for an out without any assistance from another player, the "U" symbol is used. For example, if a ground ball is hit to first base and the first baseman (only) touches the base for the out, the proper scoring is "3U."

The last scoring symbol we'll discuss is the run-batted-in (RBI). A hit ball that drives in a run is an RBI. The only times an RBI is not recorded is when an error helped the runner to score, or when a double-play enabled the runner to score. An "R" in the scoring box records a run-batted-in by the hitter. This "R" will make it easy to spot RBIs at the end of the game when you when you total the game's statistics.

Now, take some time to study Diagram 26, which shows a finished score sheet.

Now that you've had a chance to study the finished score sheet, let's review the action play-by-play (note: for simplicity, I've limited our imaginary team here to six players):

PLAYER	POS	1	2	3	4	5
SMITH	5	FC ... 2B	PB ... BB	1B	X	5U ② ... 1B
WILSON	7	4-3 ①	R ... 3B	3F ③		① SH
JONES	9	R F7 SF ②	1-3 ③	X	PB WP E-7	DP 5-3 ③
ANDERS	8	CS ③ 1B	X	R HR	F-6 ①	X
WILLIAMS	4	X	DP E-5 ①	K ①	5-3 ②	
TUCKER	2		6-4-3 DP ②	CS SB HP ②	⅄ ③	
TOTALS	R / H	1 / 2	1 / 1	1 / 1	0 / 0	0 / 1

Diagram 26
A finished score sheet

THE FIRST INNING:

Smith ledoff the first inning of the game by hitting a double (**2B**). Wilson grounded to second (**pos. 4**) and was thrown out (①) at first base (**pos. 3**). During the play, Smith moved to third on a fielder's choice (**FC**). The next batter, Jones, flied-out to left field (**F-7**) for the second out of the inning (②), but recorded an RBI when Smith scored (see the **R** in the upper corner left corner of Jones' box). Anders ended the inning with a base hit (**1B**), but was thrown out (③) attempting to steal second base (**CS**). Notice that the box of the player who would have been next at-bat is canceled with an "X" to indicate the end of the inning.

THE SECOND INNING:

The second inning started with Williams reaching first (see **blacked-out square** at the bottom right of the score box) on an error by the third baseman (**E-5**). Tucker was thrown out at first base (**pos. 3**) on his ground-ball hit to the short stop (**pos. 6**), but before he was thrown out (②), Williams was forced out (①) at second base (**pos. 4**). This play was recorded as a double play (**DP**) in both players' scoring box. Therefore, the record of this activity reads **6-4-3** in Tucker's box to accurately reflect the sequence of events.

The next hitter, Smith, was walked (**BB**) and reached second base on a passed ball (**PB**). Then, Wilson hit a triple (**3B**) which drove in Smith for an RBI (**R**). Jones ended the inning with a ground ball to the pitcher (**pos. 1**) who threw the ball to first base (**pos. 3**) for the third out (③).

THE THIRD INNING:

Anders ledoff the third inning with a home run (**HR**) which counts as an RBI (**R**). Williams struck-out swinging (**K**) for the first out (①). Tucker was hit by a pitch (**HP**) and advanced to first base. He then stole second base (**SB**) and was caught trying to steal third base (**CS**) for the second out (②). With two outs, Smith was intentionally walked (**IB**). Wilson finished the inning with a foul out (③) to first base (**pos. 3**).

THE FOURTH INNING:

Jones reached first base on an error by the left fielder (**E-7**). He ran to second base on a wild pitch (**WP**). Jones then reached third base on a passed ball (**PB**). The next hitter, Anders, hit a fly ball to the shortstop (**F-6**) for the first out (①). Williams hit a ground ball to third base (**pos. 5**) and was thrown out (②) at first base (**pos. 3**). Tucker struck out without a swing (Я) to end the fourth inning (③).

THE FIFTH INNING:

In the last inning recorded, Smith reached first base on a base hit (**1B**). Wilson bunted for a sacrifice (**SH**) and was thrown out (①), but advanced Smith to second base. Jones ended the inning with a ground ball to third base (**pos. 5**), whereby Smith was tagged out (②) by the third baseman on an unassisted play **(U5)** and Jones was thrown out **(③)** at first base **(pos. 3)** to complete the double-play **(DP)**.

Like the game of baseball itself, learning to keep score properly requires practice. Study the chart provided—or create and score your own imaginary game for extra preparation—and scoring will soon become very easy.

Equipment
Selection &
Maintenance

117

One part of the game that is often overlooked is the upkeep of equipment. Unlike many other sports, baseball does not require much equipment, but maintenance of it is still vital to the game. The most important piece of gear for a player to have and maintain is the glove. There are many types of gloves, so let's take a minute to look at the differences between them (see Figures 59–64).

When purchasing a glove you need to consider the position you'll be playing. Two specialized gloves are the catcher's mitt and the first baseman's glove (see Figures 59 and 60). A catcher's mitt is round and has a wide pocket. This glove can only be used by the catcher. It is illegal to use this glove anywhere else on the field. The first baseman's mitt is very large. It looks similar to a regular glove except that it has a rounded side on the finger portion of the glove.

Beyond these two gloves, there are a few more that are commonly used. The outfielder's glove (see Figure 61) is often the maximum glove size of thirteen inches long. The infielders' gloves (Figure 62) are sized according to the position played. The middle infielder's glove is small and short as it is especially important for the middle infielder to feel the ball in his glove and be able to get it out of the glove quickly. The third baseman's glove (Figure 63) is slightly longer than the middle infielder's glove because he has to cover the backhand play at the baseline, which requires an extended reach. He also has fewer quick-throw plays that require him to get the ball out of his glove quickly. The remaining type of glove is the pitcher's glove (Figure 64). This glove is usually medium-sized with a closed web. (A closed web is one you cannot see through.) Pitchers are not as picky as a position

Figure 59

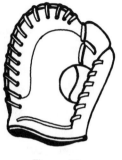

Figure 60

Figure 61

Figure 62

Figure 63

Figure 64

player when it comes to choosing a glove, and usually choose a glove based on comfort.

Once you've purchased the right glove, there are several steps you should take to maintain it, beginning with the process of breaking it in. First, simply wear your glove periodically for a few days. Play toss with the pocket of your glove. The purpose of this exercise is to draw out the oils put into the leather by the manufacturer. After working with the glove, dampen the pocket with water. This will further soften the leather and help it to conform to the shape of your hand. After a few weeks of steady play, you may need to condition the glove. In the past, players only used oil to condition the glove. Today, there are better methods. Instead of oil, use shaving lotion enriched with lanolin, applying just enough to moisten the leather. The reason for using lotion is that oil makes the glove heavy and too much oil proves difficult for the leather to absorb. By contrast, shaving lotion is very light and is easily absorbed by the leather as you rub it in.

At the end of the season, prepare your glove for winter storage by putting a ball in its pocket and tying a string or belt around it. This will help the glove to keep its form during the off-season. It's a good idea to apply a light coat of lotion at this time and store the glove in a cool, dry place.

Maintain your glove properly and you won't have to invest in a new glove every year. Do consider replacing your glove, however, when it becomes torn or too loose.

The next piece of equipment we'll discuss is footwear. Sneakers are not used in baseball because the game is played on a soft surface. Spikes are the correct shoes for baseball as sneakers will slip, causing injury. It's important to keep the bottom of the spikes clean, so make a habit of checking them every so often between innings. You'll also need to maintain your shoestrings. Laces that are too long will cause you to trip while broken laces produce a loose fit. Keep your spikes polished to repel moisture. Damp shoes often crack and quickly deteriorate.

The rules regarding spikes vary depending on the level of play. If you are playing at the lower levels (tee ball through high school) rubber spikes are most likely required. At college or higher levels, metal spikes should be worn. Be sure to check you league's rules before purchasing a new pair of shoes.

Socks are the most overlooked part of the uniform. Wearing socks incorrectly can cause foot problems and affect your play. Be sure to wear enough layers of socks so that your shoes fit tightly. If two pairs are needed, always keep two pairs handy. If one thick pair is sufficient, that's fine. Also, be sure to keep your socks dry. The goal is to avoid any condition that will cause you to slip inside your shoes.

Never wear socks that have holes in them as blisters are easy to get and painfully hard to play with. Do wear clean, white socks if for no other reason than to project a neat and professional appearance.

Another piece of equipment to consider is the bat. There is not much to maintain on the bat other than the grip, which requires that the handle be kept clean and dry. Without a good grip, hitting is very difficult. Pine tar is a great tool, but keep the tar above the handle of the bat. When using an aluminum bat, be sure the end-cap is tightly sealed. Also make certain that the cap is not cracked. When using a wood bat, inspect it regularly for chips and cracks, which will make a bat soft and cause a poor reaction of the hit ball off the bat.

When selecting a bat, you must determine the appropriate length and weight for your needs. As a general rule, the length of a bat should equal the length of your arm. Place the handle of the bat beneath your armpit and outstretch your arm. Your fingertips (only) should extend over the head of the bat. If the bat extends past your fingertips, it is too long. If most or all of your fingers extend over the bat, it is too short. Bat weight is relative to the velocity of the pitcher. Select a weight that will enable you to get your bat around on a fastball.

The following list provides an overview of additional equipment and maintenance concerns:

CATCHER'S MASK - The front cage should be solid and the straps should not be torn. Be sure the mask is adjusted correctly.

SHIN GUARDS - Check for torn straps and broken hooks.

SLIDING PANTS - These are padded pants worn under the uniform to keep legs from being torn up on a slide. Make sure the pads on these pants are still well-cushioned and sewn in place.

STIRRUPS - These are the decorative socks that come with the uniform for wear over your white socks. The elastic at the top should be in good condition.

SANITARY SOCKS - These are the thin socks worn under the stirrups. Check to see if they are stretched out or have holes.

BATTING GLOVES - Not every player uses these but if you do, check the palms for holes and pine tar build-up, and make sure the Velcro-straps are intact.

JOCK STRAP - This is the undergarment that holds the protective cup. Be sure this strap is still stretchable and that the snaps are working properly.

PROTECTIVE CUP - This is the solid protective device placed into the jock strap. Make sure the outer foam pad is not ripped and check the plastic form for cracks. Never play a game without a protective cup.

HELMET - There are two types of baseball helmets. One is the batting helmet. Be sure the ear foam and head pieces inside it are intact and inspect carefully for cracks on the outside. The other type of helmet is the catcher's helmet. Check for the same kinds of structural problems. If your model of helmet has snaps, connect the mask to the helmet to see if the snaps work.

GLOVE - We discussed maintenance of the glove at length, but for full confidence, always check the rawhide laces holding the glove together to see if they are tied tightly.

There may be other pieces of equipment used by baseball players, but these are the tools used by most. Equipment will last for many seasons and remain effective if it is maintained properly.

Coaching Strategies For Offensive & Defensive Play

The final subject covered in this book is game strategy. The coach does most of the strategizing and players carry out that strategy. The sheer number and complexity of strategies prevent a detailed discussion of each one, but we can examine a few of the strategies coaches employ in every game.

The first step is to create a strategic lineup. Most fans think that a coach puts little thought into this job, but that's not so. A coach knows that a winning lineup is important. Here's how a starting lineup is assembled:

The lead-off hitter routinely makes contact with the ball. He is usually a very fast runner and has the ability to get on base regularly. A lead-off hitter can steal and run bases better than any player on the team.

The second hitter in the order is a contact-type hitter. He is very good at bunting and seldom strikes out. The second hitter's job is to get the lead-off hitter into scoring position.

The third hitter is a power-type player. This hitter can hit homeruns and drive runners home. Most of the third hitter's at-bats are "long outs" if not a base hit.

The fourth hitter, or "clean-up hitter" as he is called, is similar to the third hitter, except his batting average may not be as high. His job is to hit home runs and drive in runs.

The fifth hitter typically makes less contact than the third and fourth hitters, but he is also a power-type hitter who has a chance to drive in runs. Generally, the fifth hitter makes the least amount of contact of those players in the middle of the lineup.

The sixth hitter can be one of two types of hitters: another power hitter who has the ability to hit fly balls, or more frequently, a line-drive-through-the-gap type hitter. This hitter has the ability to hit some home runs, but is more inclined to hit doubles. The problem with the six-hole hitter is that he has trouble with contact, so his batting average may be low.

The seventh hitter in the lineup is not usually a power hitter, but a base-hit, scrappy-type hitter. He is a fair runner but knows how to run the bases.

The eighth hitter is a fair hitter with little power. He may have home-run ability and his batting average is low. If a team has followed this formula and still has a productive hitter in this eighth position, the club is very strong.

The last hitter in the lineup is sometimes the pitcher. This hitter is usually a younger player. Occasionally, a coach will put a fast runner in this spot so he can have a player on base when the top of the order (the lead-off hitter) comes to bat.

This is only an outline of how to build a batting order. The coach can place hitters wherever he feels they will be most effective—but championship clubs usually stay close to this format.

The other coaching strategy we'll discuss is where to position players on defense. People seldom consider why players are selected to play certain positions. Diagram 28 provides a chart for the new coach to use when strategizing defensive play. It shows the positions and tools needed to play each position, with the top three tools listed regarded as the most important. The remaining tools, if a player has

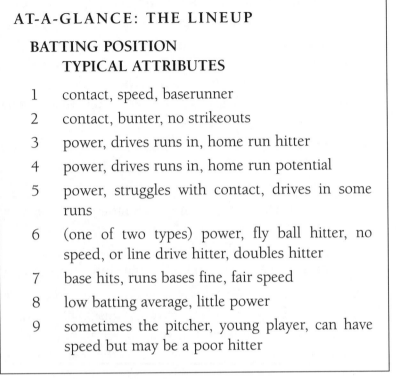

AT-A-GLANCE: THE LINEUP

BATTING POSITION
    TYPICAL ATTRIBUTES

1   contact, speed, baserunner

2   contact, bunter, no strikeouts

3   power, drives runs in, home run hitter

4   power, drives runs in, home run potential

5   power, struggles with contact, drives in some runs

6   (one of two types) power, fly ball hitter, no speed, or line drive hitter, doubles hitter

7   base hits, runs bases fine, fair speed

8   low batting average, little power

9   sometimes the pitcher, young player, can have speed but may be a poor hitter

Diagram 27

them, are considered an added bonus. Keep in mind, however, that the pitcher's tools are treated differently than the position players' tools, and that a team seldom has players with all the skills needed to fulfill their position's ideal requirements.

Before reviewing the chart, let's examine the tools a player needs to play the game of baseball.

1. Arm strength - the ability to throw the ball hard and accurately.

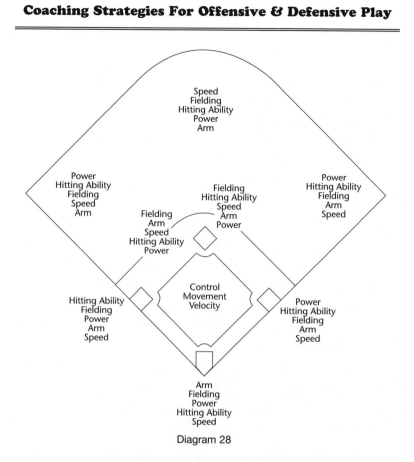

Diagram 28

2. Fielding ability - the ability to catch all balls thrown and hit.

3. Running speed - the ability to run fast, needed for both baserunning and running down balls hit while playing defense.

4. Hitting ability - the ability to make contact and put the ball in play when at bat.

5. Power - the ability to hit long home runs and drive the ball into the outfield when at bat.

These five tools are the stock of a good baseball player. It is not mandatory for a player to have all these tools, but the more a player has, the greater his potential.

At the beginner level, this chart may not hold true, but as a player advances in skill and experience, he will have to determine the position at which he is most likely to excel. The following summary of Diagram 28 may help you to make this decision.

The Left Fielder is usually a power-type hitter. He is a fair fielder with enough arm strength to reach the cutoff man, and in most cases, he is a fair runner.

The Center Fielder is the fastest on the team, a lead-off-type hitter with baserunning ability. Because the left and right fielders are only fair defensive players, the center fielder must be an excellent fielder. A center fielder's arm strength is not especially important, but it's nice to have.

The Right Fielder, like the left fielder, is another power hitter. His tools are similar except he has more arm strength.

The Third Baseman plays a position that requires good hitting and fielding abilities. Range is not as important as quickness. Arm strength is a real asset but it's not the most important tool.

The Shortstop is usually the best infielder on defense. He has outstanding fielding skills, especially in terms of his ability to run and throw. This position is farthest from first base, so arm strength is required. This player must also cover the most ground to make plays, so running speed is important, too. A shortstop must be, in essence, a coach on the field.

The Second Baseman has much the same tools as the shortstop, except he may have greater hitting ability and a little less arm strength. Most second basemen can play shortstop in an emergency.

The First Baseman is a reliable power-hitter with limited defensive skills. Most first basemen have fair arms and do not run well. If a first baseman can also field well, it's a real plus.

The Catcher has to be a very good defensive player because runners often steal bases and pitchers do not always throw strikes. He must also have a strong arm and be able to throw accurately—especially when attempting to throw out a runner stealing a base. It is not especially important that a catcher hit well, but it's nice to have a power hitter in this position.

The Pitcher has a position unlike any other. A pitcher's main purpose is to get hitters out. Therefore, he must be able to throw strikes. Of course, a strong arm is very useful here but it's not the most important tool needed to get hitters out. Movement on the pitch is more valuable than speed. If a pitcher has control, combined with movement and velocity, he is an outstanding pitcher. Speed alone is nice, but without the other capabilities it is of little use in consistently striking out hitters.

Glossary

COMMON BASEBALL TERMS AND RULES OF THE GAME

There are many terms and regulations that apply to the game of baseball. While this section will provide you with an overview of the most common terms and general rules, keep in mind that every level of baseball (e.g., Little League) has its own interpretation of the rules, so be sure to consult the correct rule book. Symbols for scoring are noted in parentheses.

ALTERED BAT - A bat is considered altered (and therefore, illegal) when it has been changed from its original form. Examples are: taping a broken bat, filling or emptying an aluminum bat, and cutting a wooden bat to size.

BALK (BK) - An illegally thrown pitch. For example, a pitcher throws a pitch without his foot being in contact with the rubber. The penalty for a balk is that all runners advance one base.

BASE LINE - The line a runner must use to get from base to base. If no line is drawn, then a three-foot imaginary line is used (see Figure 65).

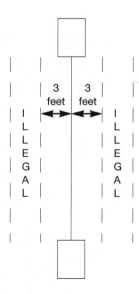

Figure 65

BATTING ORDER - This is sometimes called a lineup and consists of the official roster of players listed in the order they will hit during the game. The list must be provided to the umpire before the start of the game.

BUNT - A pitched ball that is tapped into play by a hitter, instead of hit with a full swing. A ball that is hit with a full swing and travels a very short distance is sometimes called a swinging bunt (see Figure 66).

CALL - A loud exclamation made by a position player when he feels he can make the play on a fly ball *("I got it!"* or *"Ball!"* or *"Me!"*).

Figure 66

CALL-OFF - A player's indication that he is *not* making the catch on a fly ball, shouted to the player whom will make the play *("You take it!"* or an exclamation of the other player's name or position).

CATCH - A ball that is caught in the glove or bare hand of a defensive player with enough control to transfer the ball to someone else (see Figures 67, 68).

CATCH & CARRY - This is a legal catch that is carried by the player into foul territory. All runners are then awarded one base, unless instructed otherwise by the officials.

CHECK SWING - This occurs when the hitter changes his mind about the pitch and stops his swing before it crosses the plate. If the bat crosses the plate, a full swing is called (see Figure 69).

Figure 67

CLEAR THE BAG - An action taken by the position player covering the base to move a safe distance away from the bag to make a throw or to continue the play.

Figure 68

CLEAR THE RUNNER - An evasive action taken by the position player to avoid an oncoming runner.

CROW HOP - The small jump used to gain momentum before making a throw.

CUTOFF PLAY - A relay of the ball in situations where a throw of great distance requires the assistance of another player to make an additional throw.

DEAD BALL - Any ball touched or influenced by something or

Figure 69

135

someone outside of the rules of the game may be ruled out-of-play or "dead."

DELIVERY - A term used for that part of the pitching action whereby the ball is thrown to home plate.

DISLODGED BASE - A base that has broken loose during the course of the game. All bases are to be mounted to the ground before the start of the game; any base moved during a play must be remounted in its original position.

DOUBLE (2B) - A hit that enables the hitter to reach second base safely and without the benefit of an error by the defense.

DOUBLE PLAY (DP) - A play by the defense where two outs are made on one pitched ball.

DRAG BUNT - A bunt specifically intended to achieve a base hit (unlike the sacrifice bunt which is intended only to advance the runner already on base).

DUGOUT - An out-of-play area reserved for the team and its equipment.

EJECTION - When a player or coach is disqualified by an umpire for committing an illegal act during the game. This act may take place on or off the field.

ENGLISH - The spin on a ball that causes it to move in an odd motion when it rolls on the ground.

ERROR (E) - A mistake: a ball that is thrown so poorly it cannot be caught, or a hit ball that should have been fielded and was not, are common errors. It is the scorekeeper's job to call an error. As a general rule, any play that the average fielder should make and for some reason does not make is called an error.

FAIR BALL - A batted ball that is ruled by the umpire as inside the field of play. It is not mandatory, however, that the ball stay in fair territory for the entire play.

FAIR TERRITORY - The area marked by the white line on the field. The line starts at the point of home plate and extends down the first and third baselines to the foul poles (see Diagram 29).

FAKE TAG - This type of tag is illegal at most levels and occurs when a defensive player pretends to have the ball and touches the runner to slow him down.

Foul Pole

Foul Pole

Fair Territory

Foul Territory

Fair Territory

Fair Territory

Foul Territory

Diagram 29

FIELDER'S CHOICE (FC) - A scoring term that indicates that a hitter has reached a base or a runner has advanced a base because the fielder decided to put out another runner instead.

FINISH/FOLLOW THROUGH - The ending of a pitcher's delivery to the plate, which includes the movement of the pitcher's arms and legs after the ball has been released from his hand.

FLY BALL OUT (F) - A scoring term that indicates a ball hit in the air and caught in the field of play.

FORCE OUT - An out made without having to tag the runner with the ball. Force plays usually occur at first base, but can happen any time a runner must move to the next base because another runner is attempting the base he's on.

FOUL BALL - Any ball hit by the batter that lands in the area outside the fair territory. If a ground ball lands in a foul area first and returns to fair territory before it passes the bases, it is a fair ball. If a ball is touched by the defense in foul ground before it passes the base, however, it is ruled foul. Any ball entering the field of play on the ground beyond the base is foul (see Diagram 30).

FOUL TIP - A ball struck by

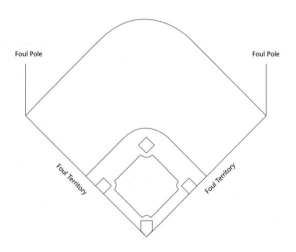

Diagram 30

the bat during a swing which neither travels any distance nor enters fair territory.

HIT BY PITCH (HP) - A scoring term which indicates that a batter was struck by a pitched ball while at bat. This designation does not apply to a hitter struck by a pitched ball while attempting a swing.

HOME RUN (HR) - 1. A ball hit through fair territory over the fence. 2. A ball hit far enough into fair territory for the hitter to score without the benefit of an error by the fielders. This is called an in-the-park home run.

HOME TEAM - The team that bats second following the start of the game. In leagues where teams travel to games, the non-traveling team is dubbed the home team.

HOT SHOT - A term used for a ball hit hard and traveling at a high speed, usually directly toward a position player.

INFIELD FLY - When caught, this is an automatic out. An infield fly occurs when a fly ball is hit to the infielders while runners are on first and second, or bases are full with less than two outs. The batter is automatically out and the runners do not have to advance. This rule was instated to keep the infielders from dropping the ball on purpose in order to get two outs instead of one. The hit ball does not have to stay in the infield—but an infielder has to make the catch.

INTENTIONAL WALK (IB) - A scoring term that indicates that a pitcher decided to walk a hitter because he felt he could not strike him out, or because he believed it was to his advantage to face (pitch to) the next hitter instead.

INTERFERENCE - This is called when a baserunner, hitter, or fielder gets in the way of a play being made: A hitter must stay out of the way of a player making the play on a hit or thrown ball, a runner must stay clear of a fielder making a play, and a fielder must stay clear of the baseline while a runner is trying to advance to another base (see Figures 70, 71).

Figure 70

Figure 71

LEGAL TAG - This occurs when a runner or batter is not touching a base when a fielder who has possession of the hit or thrown ball touches the baserunner or hitter (see Figure 72).

LONG HOP - The action taken by a ball that bounces far enough in front of a player that he can catch it waist-high after the bounce.

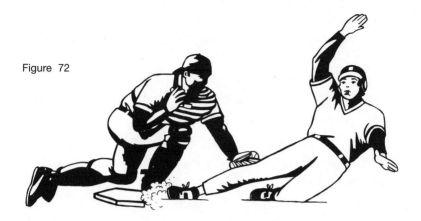

Figure 72

LONG OUT - A term used for a fly ball hit deep into the outfield. Often, this ball looks like a home run when it is hit but it falls short of the fence and is caught by the fielder.

MECHANICS - The order and approach a player takes to conduct his movement. Any time a player reacts to a situation, he uses some sort of mechanics to get his body in position to succeed.

MOVEMENT - The action of the ball when it is thrown. Side-to-side movement is known as "tail" or "run." Downward movement is called "sink" and upward movement is called "jumping" or "riding."

OBSTRUCTION - There are two types of obstruction: when a defensive player interferes with a hitter trying to hit a pitched ball (usually called catcher's interference), or when a fielder not holding or trying to field the ball gets in the way of the runner (usually called interference, see above).

OVERTHROW - An overthrow is committed when a thrown ball is tossed over or past a fielder into a foul- or dead-ball area. If runners are on base when a ball is tossed into a dead-ball area, runners advance to the base they were attempting plus one additional base. If the ball was overthrown from the mound, only one base is awarded.

PASSED BALL (PB) - A legally pitched ball that was missed by the catcher. This ruling is made by the scorekeeper. A runner must advance a base for a passed ball to be called. If no runner advances, a passed ball is not awarded.

PICK UP - A directive that urges one to look *for* or *at* (a person or the ball). For instance, to pick up the target or ball means to look at. To pick up the base coach means to look for him for advice or information.

POP UP - A fly ball which travels a short distance to the infield or the catcher (a pop up could be caught by an outfielder, but close to the infield).

PROTEST - This occurs when a manager or coach disagrees with a ruling (not a judgement call) and asks league officials to review the call. There are three instances when a protest can be lodged:

a when the umpire's decision contradicts the rule book;

b when a player is substituted or re-entered in the game illegally; and

c when an ineligible player is put into the game.

Protests must also be timed proper to the alleged violation: in (a), a protest must be made before the next pitch; in (b), a protest must be made while the player is in the game; and in (c), a protest can be made during or after the game.

ROUNDING THE BAG - The route a baserunner takes when running past a base with the intention of proceeding to the next base. Instead of making a sharp left turn at every base, a runner will advance at a slightly rounded angle into each base.

RUN BATTED IN (RBI) - A scoring term used to credit to the hitter the number runs scored by baserunners as a direct result of his hit.

RUNNER PICKED OFF BASE (PO) - A scoring term that indicates that a runner was tagged out without a hit (or any contact with the ball) being made by the hitter; rather, the ball was thrown to the base and the runner was tagged out because he was off-base (while taking a lead, for example).

SACRIFICE BUNT (SH) - A bunt which is solely intended to advance the runner on base. This bunt is not made to achieve a single. A bunt intended to produce a single is called a drag bunt.

SACRIFICE FLY (SF) - This is a statistical rule that applies when a batter brings in a run on a fly ball with fewer than two outs. A sacrifice fly does not occur when a runner simply advances a base—he must score on the fly ball.

SHORT HOP - The action taken by a ball when it is thrown or bounces very close to the fielder, thereby making it hard to catch or field. A short hop will require a fielder to make the play below his knees and possibly cause him to lose sight of the ball.

SHOVEL TOSS - A short throw which is made by under-handing the ball to the other player, who is typically within a few steps of the player making the toss.

SINGLE (1B) - When a hitter hits the ball and reaches first base safely without the occurrence of an error by the defense.

SLOW ROLLER - a ball that is swung at and hit, which travels a short distance at a relatively slow speed in fair territory. This ball can be fielded by a player without his glove because it is traveling so slowly.

SOFT HANDS - A term that describes the smooth technique with which a player catches the ball. Good fielders usually catch the ball as if it were breakable and are said to have "soft hands."

SQUARE-UP - The act of positioning the body in the proper position to throw to the next player. This position always involves having a clear view of the intended target.

STEALING - When a runner advances a base without a hit, walk, or passed ball. A steal is not awarded on a wild or illegal pitch. A stolen base is indicated on the score sheet with the letters "SB." A runner caught stealing is indicated with the letters "CS."

STRIKEOUT (K or backwards K) - When a hitter swings and misses three pitches during an at-bat. A backwards K is recorded in the score book when the third strike was not swung at by the hitter.

STRIKE ZONE - Once the batter takes his accustomed stance at the plate, any ball that crosses the plate below the batter's armpits and above the top of his knees is considered to be within this zone (see Diagram 31).

Diagram 31

TAIL - A term that refers to the typical side-to-side movement of the pitched ball. Tail is also known as "run."

145

TAKE OUT/TAKEN OUT - When a runner slides into the base in manner that causes the position player to jump away or fall in order to avoid a collision (thereby preventing him from making an additional throw), it is said that the position player is "taken out."

TRAPPED BALL - A fly ball or line drive that hits the ground or fence before being caught by a defensive player. This situation happens so quickly that a trapped ball may appear to be a catch—but it is not.

TRIPLE PLAY (3B) - A play by the defense where three outs are made on one pitched ball. In a triple play, the outs do not have to occur in any specific order.

UNASSISTED PLAY (U) - A scoring term that indicates that a defensive player succeeded in putting out two runners on one hit ball without the assistance of any other player.

WALK (BB) - When the umpire rules four pitches as being out of the strike zone during one at-bat, that player at bat is awarded (walks to) first base.

WILD PITCH (WP) - A thrown, legal pitch that cannot be caught by the catcher. As with an error, a wild pitch is judged as such according to the average catcher's ability.

WIND-UP - The action taken by a pitcher from the start of the pitch to the point of the ball's release. Every pitch to the plate requires some manner of wind up.